SCHOOL
OF
MONEY

"Learn what schools will never teach you about money"

MICHAEL EDIALE

I dedicate this book to the millions of people all over the world who are serious to take charge of their financial education to attain financial freedom.

PREFACE

I have wondered and pondered for years about the reason why many people struggle financially working hard all their lives for money for years and discovered from personal experience and reading numerous books and articles on the subject of wealth accumulation and realized that been rich or poor is a matter of choice.

The root of our economic and financial problem is traceable to the school which has failed in teaching people how to make money rather than working for money. Most people graduate from school to become employees who have been trained with the mindset of working hard for money all their lives. Many people have vowed to die in job security, working for a pay money because that is the only method they know about making money.

This lack of money problem has become a national and international problem that affects the world. It is the inability of financial education and intelligence in the world that has contributed to the high rate of poverty affecting us all. As prophet Hosea put it so eloquently; " My people perish for lack of knowledge." The key to unlock and enjoy financial independence is acquiring the skills and understanding how the system of making money works. This requires a long time process of continuous learning. It requires no higher academic qualification and display of genius to become a master in the art of money making. Submit your self to apprenticeship and open your mind to reality.

The more you get informed the better equipped you are to become prosperous. The higher your financial intelligence the more powerful you are to survive in both good and bad times.

Education is meant to add value into lives and help you maximize your potentials. Financial education is essential to our well-being as individuals and our nation. This book is not a get rich quick book but a life changing book that will change the way you think about money , life and success. I don't blame the traditional school system for not teaching you how to make money.

I passed through school without been taught how to make money but work hard for money. A change in my thought , changed my reality. If the school educated only the head, this book will educate your mind and empower you to make wealth which is the secret to financial security .

By purchasing this book or downloading the e-book is the greatest thing that you have done towards investing in your financial education. As you read this book and digest the principles your life will undergo a series of mental transformation through the right path to success and gain the secrets of creating and accumulating lasting wealth.   I hope to see you over the top. It's time for financial education.

- Michael Ediale

"Education is the best provision for old age."
-Aristotle

PART ONE

MONEY

WON'T MAKE YOU RICH

"Practice the reality principle; deal with the world as it is, not as you wish it would be."

- Jack Welch

Many people have been deceived and will remain slaves working hard for money all their lives because of the false believe that money will make them rich. If you should ask me if money can make you rich? I would simple tell you no! Money can't make you rich. I know people who earn money from high paying jobs, working daily for money yet they are struggling financially, failing to get richer. If money alone makes someone rich why do we have millionaires who have gone bankrupt, politicians looting funds, lottery winners going broke to become poor again. It is not the amount of money that you have piled in your bank account that determines how richer you will become in life but it is about the idea that you have about the money that counts.

IDEA MAKE YOU RICH

Money is an idea. It is the idea that you have about money that determines how richer you will become in life. People without ideas can't make money. They can only work hard for money than their money work hard for them. If you lack ideas for something, you are ignorant. An ignorant person knows nothing about something. Ideas are products of knowledge . Without the proper application of knowledge about money people will keep struggling financially. It is about the idea not just about the money.

GETTING RICH QUICK

The getting rich quick syndrome is a disease like cancer that can begin with a single cell, or an opportunity to make and get free money quickly. Most people have been programmed right from school to compete for grades which would make them rich in the real world. I have seen students wishing to study and graduate with good grades to get a high paying job that will make them get rich quick. There is no magic formula for getting rich quick. You can't find it in this book. This book will take you through the process of learning what the schools failed to teach you about making money. Which you can apply in your life to become successful.

DID YOUR PARENTS TEACH YOU ABOUT MONEY?

Our first teachers were our parents. It is through them that we came into life. Whatever values and lessons they taught us helped in sharpening our future and destiny. It's sad enough to know that most parents are struggling financially. They only know how to work hard for money to fend for their families. I have seen parents lure their children into paths that they never desire. Just to go and work for money and get instant gratification. Most parents are encouraging their children and become wage slaves by telling them to school, get good grades and get a high paying job after graduation. Most parents invest their hard earned money in their children's lives. With the impression that when they grow old their children would take care of them. That is the mentality of the poor and middle class. Education and high paying jobs matters much to them. They value job security to financial security.What your parents teach you about money becomes a reality of who you become. If they told you that the love of money is evil, you will not have the drive and desire to make money. If you were told that working for money by clinging to job security is the only way to become rich. You will desire to become a working wage slave. My father worked for money all his life and died as an employee to the Nigerian Railway Corporation. While my mother was an entrepreneur with chains of business. She worked on building assets that worked hard to generate money for her. She is late, but her business lives as it is been passed down to her children.

BEWARE WHAT YOUR TEACHERS TEACH YOU

Who are your teachers and what do they teach you about money? Teachers are employees trained to work hard for money they will only teach you how they work hard for money as they were trained. Most people are been left behind financially because of how they were trained and what they were taught by their teachers. Teachers like loyalty, they reward loyal students who will listen to them and carry out their instructions and punish those that won't just like me. While in school I had problem with my teachers just because I refused to accept what they told me. I failed to pass the West African Examination Council Examination for about five times just because I refused to answer the questions they way they wanted it. After graduation I refused to work for anybody simple because I hate taking orders and been told what to do. If you want to work hard for money all your life you need to be loyal to what you were been taught by your teachers and be loyal employee to your boss. I am sure most people are now regretting following their teachers advice which has led them into a financial shipwreck.

ARE YOU OBSOLLETE?

The world is changing rapidly before our very eyes. The shift in the world is creating more opportunities and problems for many people economically and financially. In the industrial age it use to be wars of missile but in the information age its now war of speed modem. The rules of money have changed leaving people struggling financially behind. Working hard and save money to become rich is an old advice which has destroyed the lives and mortgage the financial well-being of many people. The new rule is working smart and invest. It requires financial intelligence to apply these new rule.

FEAR FACTOR

Fear is a major obstacle to achieving success. People who are afraid to go out of the comfort zone of job security to tap into the unlimited opportunities under their feet and face challenges will prefer to work hard for money and feel comfortable with their jobs. Fear of failure is a cause of poverty. People who are afraid to start a business or invest are afraid of taking risk. They are afraid of losing money and making a mistake. This emotional aspect of fear is sabotaging them from actualizing financial mastery over their life. To become financial successful you must exterminate the fear factor from your mind and be prepared to explore into a new world of great wealth opportunities. Frankline D. Roosevelt rightfully advised; *"There is nothing to fear but fear itself."*

MISTAKES MAKE YOU GREAT

A man that is afraid of making mistakes will never achieve anything great. Show me a loser and I will show you an excuser. Mistakes are considered a sacrilege in school. Students that make most of the mistakes in school are penalized and rewarded with poor grades. In real world mistakes are what make men great. Thomas Edison 10,000 mistakes made him great. Show me a man with mistakes and I will show you a great man. I love making mistakes that is why I never bothered to work for any one. No one will want to employ someone like me. Mistakes are meant to corrected and there are great lessons that are to be learned. If not for the mistakes that I did to fail English language and mathematics five times in the West African Examination Council I wouldn't have become an international selling author today. And probably you wouldn't have been reading this book now. Mistakes brought out the real me. I discovered my true potentials and strength from making mistakes. I have started business and failed, each time I fail I realize the better I become.

A journalist once interviewed Thomas J. Watson Sr, the founder of IBM, how he could be more successful faster . Watson replied with these beautiful words; *" If you want to be successful faster, you must double your rate of failure. Success lies on the far side of failure."*

FALSE ASSUMPTION

Believing that it takes money to make money is mediocre philosophy. You can lose money in anything and your money can stop flowing in once your working days are over or you are fired. It is your financial intelligence that would make you more richer than been a wage worker. I have seen people that pill gold without knowing anything about what to do with the gold. I have seen people saving money thinking that is the best investment without risk not knowing that is the most riskiest and foolish decision to make.

WORKING HARD VS WORKING SMART

Most middle class and poor think working hard is the best way to get out of debt and attain financial security. People that work hard, earn hard and live hard all their lives. Working smart people achieve financial success, having time for themselves and families making their money work hard for them without stress. Working hard people live bellow their means and working smart people expand their means. This requires financial intelligence.

THE BEST DESCISION THAT I HAVE MADE

Many people are looking for someone to invest in their ideas and their lives. When they have not invested in themselves by acquiring the financial intelligence and experience they need to survive in this competitive world. The best investment that I have ever made in my life is to invest in my personal development and financial knowledge within the years. It's a continuous process there is no day of graduation. The day you stop learning is the day you stop dying. You learn to earn. I rather spend my time and money to learn how to make money through buying books , audio and video CDs and attending seminars than work for money all my life.

KEY POINTS

- ✓ It is not the amount of money that you have piled in your bank account that determines how richer you will become in life but it is about the idea that you have about the money that counts.
- ✓ Without the proper application of knowledge about money people will keep struggling financially. It is about the idea not just about the money.
- ✓ What your parents teach you about money becomes a reality of who you become. If they told you that the love of money is evil, you will not have the drive and desire to make money. If you were told that working for money by clinging to job security is the only way to become rich. You will desire to become a working wage slave.
- ✓ Most people are been left behind financially because of how they were trained and what they were taught by their teachers.
- ✓ Working hard people live bellow their means and working smart people expand their means.

PART TWO

FINANCIAL INTELLIGENCE IS THE KEY

" You can never lose anything that really belongs to you, and you can't keep that which belongs to someone else."

- Edgar Cayce

-

TYPES OF INTELLIGENCE?

Academic Intelligence
Professional Intelligence
Financial Intelligence

ACCADEMIC INTELLIGENCE

Academic intelligence is what the school impart into the lives of students. Students go to school to learn how to read, write and solve mathematical problems. This kind of intelligence is measured by grades. This is what the school make many people to believe is a basic requirement for success in life which is not true. I am not saying that academic intelligence is bad what I am trying to say is that it limits people's ability to discover and maximize their potentials as their lives are been governed by grades and portfolio of credential. Most people that like this form of intelligence spend their working life around the academic circle acquiring more higher qualification, competing for grades and salaries as teacher, lectures and professors. This form of intelligence train people as employees to get jobs and work for money for years and retire. I have seen smart academia's and book smart people brag about their high qualifications with no money to show. I have seen school dropouts and illiterates employ them to work for them. It requires more than academic intelligence to survive in today's volatile world of job insecurity.

PROFESSIONAL INTELLIGENCE

This form of intelligence train people to become professionals. Learning a skill that will be paid for.

For example lawyers attend law school to become lawyers, doctors attend medical school to become doctors. Most people with this form of intelligence become partial employees , consultants and self employed. They charge higher fees and run their show alone. They have a problem of expanding and involving many people into their business. They prefer doing things their way and believing that their way is often the right way to do things. This form of intelligence is for someone that wants to skip the rat race of job security as an employee to establish his firm but affiliated with a union. They think it's a smart career to become self employed yet they have the mindset of employees. They still work hard for money so they are not out of the rat race even if they are minding their business.

FINANCIAL INTELLIGENCE

The rich focuses on financial intelligence and academic intelligence. While the poor and middle class focuses on academic intelligence and professional intelligence. Financial intelligence is the product of wealth accumulation and creation of the rich. It is a great asset that rich leverage upon. If you don't have academic and professional intelligence but you spend years and time to acquire financial intelligence you will become richer than people with academic and professional intelligence. Financial intelligence is a great advantage edge against people that depend on their academic and professional credentials to become richer. Every skill is learnable , to learn the skill of money making can be learned just like any other skill that you can ever imagine.

MONEY PROBLEMS

Money problem is what affects the rich, poor, middle class, country, government and church. Everybody solves their money problem differently and react differently. While the poor and middle class complain and blame the government and their employers for their money problems and seldom keep their money problems to themselves and allow their problems to consume them. The rich look for smart people to solve their money problems. Financial intelligence will help you solve your financial problem creatively. You need to be smart in solving your money problem.

TOO MUCH MONEY

If you don't have money it's a problem and if you have too much money it's a bigger problem. Everybody desires to become a millionaire, bust sustaining the status quo of been a millionaire is more challenging than having the millions. You need to continue increasing your financial intelligence , passing through the process and learning to master your money skill.

MONEY DOES NOT SOLVE PROBLEMS

To think that it takes money to solve money problems is a mediocre thinking. Many people believe that if they have all the money in the world their financial problems will be solved. That's not true, having lots of money causes more problems. Money alone doesn't solve financial problems it only prolongs the problems and creates more poor people. Take for example people cry for pay rise, expect money form the government through social welfare programs to alleviate poverty and cling to higher paying jobs. This encourages laziness and declines initiative. It doesn't take money to make money it takes idea to make money and idea to solve money problems through financial smartness.

HARD WORK DOESN'T SOLVE MONEY PROBLEMS

Hard work doesn't solve money problem. The more hard working you become they more harder your money problems. I have seen people jump from job to job working hard to solve their financial problems. The world is filled with hard working people who earn money, yet grow deeper in debt, working harder for more money. Hard work doesn't solve money problems, brain work makes the magic.

JUST OVER BROKE

Are you just over broke? Just over broke means J.O.B the world is filled with people who value job security than financial security. There is really no security in a job. The day you are laid off or retrenched the party is up. Many educated people think having a high paying job can solve their financial problems. They earn just enough to survive but cannot afford to live. Most people can't even set aside enough money for retirement, health care and fend for their families.

JOB SECURITY VS FINANCIAL SECURITY

There are two methods to solve money problems. Many people prefer job security than financial security. The world is changing rapidly the hope for job security is becoming obsolete. People are been pushed out of their comfort walls of security into the real challenging world without any plan put in place taking care of them. Depending on someone to take care of your financial problem is a fairy tale in this dispensation. You need to grow up and take responsibility for your life and solve your financial problems. Both Job and financial security are not the best methods of solving financial problems. Security means to be secured. You are either trapped in job security or financial security. The freedom that comes in having mastery over our money and life is the creative ability of solving money problems and challenges.

WHAT SOLVES MONEY PROBLEMS?\

Financial intelligence solves money problems. It constitute part of our intelligence used to solve financial problems. If our financial intelligence is low it would affect our ability to solve money problems. It requires development of the intelligence. I might want to buy a car and not have the money the power of financial intelligence will help me solve the problem of not having money to buy the car to afford the car within a stipulated period of time.

BECOME A SMART PROBLEM SOLVER

When you begin to solve your personal money problems you will get smarter. This will increase your financial intelligence and make you richer beyond your wildest dreams. You inability to solve your financial problems makes you poorer. Problems are contagious and cancerous. Any little problem grows into more bigger problem if not solved. Financial intelligence empowers you to become a smart problem solver not a problem maker. If you can't solve your money problem you can't get rich and quit financial struggle. The longer the problem persist , the poorer you will become. Its just like ignoring a little weed that will soon grow bigger into a bush around your house inviting snakes and rodents.

THE ROOT OF POVERTY

Poverty creates more problems than solutions. People who experience poverty simply have bigger problems that they can't solve. Lack of financial intelligence and education to solve small problems grow into full blown poverty. A nation that fails to solve its financial problem will become a bankrupt poverty ridden poor economic nation. The right way to escape poverty is to continual learn ,develop and increase ones financial intelligence. As prophet Hosea said; " My people perish for lack of knowledge." In this context I will put it this way; " My people perish for lack of financial knowledge."

LEARN FROM THE RICH

The rich have their rules of solving money problems. The learn to watch for changes in the economy, laws , policies and seasons. A change in the world makes more people richer and more people poorer. The rich values financial intelligence than any other form of intelligence. It is through these medium that they are able to solve their problems and get richer. The higher their financial intelligence , the bigger the problems they can handle. The rich see financial challenges as opportunities to become smart problem solver to become richer . Instead of looking for someone to blame and cast the problem to they face their problems and get richer in the process. The poor see money problem as problems. They whine and complain as if they are the only ones with money problems. They think having more money will solve their problem. Their inability to solve their problem on escalates their money problem. They increase their financial weakness and ignore their financial strength.

THE BEST EDUCATION I EVER HAD

I acquired academic education but it never constituted to my success in life. While starting out I had no money and wasn't born with a silver spoon. I never applied for a job to work for money. Many people thought I was insane, I can't survive without money. Families redrew their support for me, friends jeered at me. Thinking I was wasting my life and time. I refused to stop 2 + 2 that I was taught in school I went further to think out of the box to solve my financial problem.

I spent years in upgrading and refining my financial intelligence through books, articles and Audio Cds. I invested every penny I had to acquire this great education that exposed me to a world of great opportunities and possibilities to succeed. If I want to start a business now I can boldly start it without money and make my vision a reality. Lack of money had never stopped me from achieving any of my desired goal. I have seen young entrepreneurs say they have great ideas for products and services but lack of money is stopping them. He who has the gold makes the rules. I have the financial intelligence to get my gold and make my rules. The best education that I have ever had is financial education which I recommend also for you. If I hadn't opened my mind and invested in my financial education. I would have been wiped out long ago.

KEY POINTS

- ✓ Financial intelligence is the product of wealth accumulation and creation of the rich. It is a great asset that rich leverage upon.
- ✓ You need to be smart in solving your money problem.
- ✓ Hard work doesn't solve money problems, brain work makes the magic.
- ✓ Financial intelligence empowers you to become a smart problem solver not a problem maker.

✓ If you can't solve your money problem you can't get rich and quit financial struggle.

✓ The right way to escape poverty is to continual learn ,develop and increase ones financial intelligence.

✓ The best education that I have ever had is financial education which I recommend also for you.

PART THREE

UNLOCKING SECRETS
FINANCIAL
INTELLIGENCE

"Events are influenced by our great desires."
- William James

WHAT SCHOOL CALLS FINANCIAL EDUCTION

While in school, some men dressed in suit will be invited by the school to come and give a talk to the students. Advising us to get good grades to get high paying jobs, cultivate a high saving attitude and become financially free. Many people that had followed this advice are regretting today. In my book Naira Crisis I called wrote about wolves in sheep clothing. These con men from the banks are already preparing the mindset of young students to graduate, get a job and turn over their money to them. That is the monkey been trained to throw bananas to baboons. Many people are still cultivating this habit of working hard and turning their hard earned income into their bank accounts thinking they are smart with their money.

ONCE A FOOL

The world is filled with desperate people who are willing and ready to help you take care of your money if you don't know what to do with it. When I wanted to start a business of producing and selling a audio compilation of music. I had a friend who is a DJ called mummy's pet. I gave him money to record and produce the audio compilation and print the jacket for me he took very good care of my money as he wasted my time for six months without delivering what I gave him money to do. He used my money to handle his stomach problem. I had to involve the police before I could recover part of the money from him. I failed to learn my lesson from the previous experience I had with him. I once hosted a musical show he flopped everything by spending the money I gave him to pay the invited artistes and rent equipments. I thought I could trust him but he betrayed my trust. He extorted me in whatever way he could just to help me take care of my money. Then I was a financial moron and I was treated like a moron. There are people that are looking for a way to cheat and steal the little money that you have. One of the easiest way of stealing money with your cooperation is by depositing your money in a bank. While they are telling you; " Thanks for depositing your money with us." They are indirectly telling you they will really take care of your money. You will learn what to do with your money in subsequent chapters of this book.

WHO CONTROLS YOUR MONEY

Are you in control of your money? Or someone helps you to control your money. Academic and professional intelligence prepares your life to be controlled. The money you earned is controlled and the place that it goes to is beyond your control. This is financial bondage. " No man is free who cannot control himself." As Pluto observed. If you have no freedom to control your money then you are not free. Its either someone is in control or your are a slave to your money. Financial intelligence empowers you to have total control over your money than over yourself. Financial independence cannot be achieved without financial intelligence. You are either a master or a slave over your money. A master controls while a slave works. When you work hard for money you are enslaved to money. I don't need anybody to tell me what to do with my money. I tell my money what it should do for me and its working hard for me.

FINANCIAL PRISON

Many people are trapped in financial prison. They are victims of money problems. No matter how they work hard and save hard the still live hard bellow their means. Many people think that they are smart they get higher qualifications, get a secured job. They save to buy a house and car and compete to climb the cooperate lather. They think their retirement benefits and saved money in their bank accounts is enough to insulate them from the cruel world of not having enough money. They think they are financially free while ironically they are trapped in a financial prison. There is no freedom in working for money all the days of your life. They lack adequate financial education to attain financial freedom that is why they prefer financial security than face their financial challenges. Instead of starting a business, they help people run their business, instead of making their money, they help someone to work for money all their lives. After retirement they are lost in the world of job insecurity and end up wallowing in abject penury and poverty.

RISK THE RISK

Working for money is riskier than making money. The things you risk are the things that become risky. Taking risk has a potential effect to make you rich and afraid of taking risk has a potential effect to make you and keep you poor. People who are comfortable with financial security are cowards who are avoid the wonderful challenges in the real world.

WORDS ARE POWERFUL

Don't underestimate the power of words. Words have life and they are flesh. You can distinguish a poor person and a rich person from the kind of words they use. Your words sharpen who you become. Most people are poor because of their words which complements their actions. You can know a rich person from the kind of words they use and it complements their action. Poor people think and talk small while rich people think big and talk big. I don't care if you think its pride but you have to be proud of who you are or you would remain where you are. I once visited a barbing saloon and the barber was ridiculing me that I am broke. I reversed and refused to accept what he told me. I fired back at him that I am rich , a billionaire. That was the last time I ever stepped my feet there. What people tell you has a potential effect in sharpening your future and destiny. Reject every negative talk and think positively. What you think about becomes a reality which constitutes your success in life.

A WAY OF THINKING

Riches and poverty is a way of thinking not about the amount of money in your pocket. The rich and the poor think differently and act differently. If you think you can't afford it or do it your thinking will work for or against you. In my first book Think like the rich I explained the power of thoughts and how your thinking can make you successful and happy in life. Get it to read on amazon.com to become rich is about having a right mental attitude. "There is nothing that can help a man with a wrong mental attitude, but there is something that can help a man with a positive mental attitude." As James Jefferson asserted. If you want to attain financial freedom easier the first step is to change what you think about money.

CHOICES

Life is filled with abundant choices. The choices that we make is what our lives become. I have made a choice in my life to become rich. I wasn't born with a silver spoon I have to create my silver spoon. I have battled with poverty and experienced penury rather than given up I kept fighting to rise above poverty. I am the last son of my family, my father had two wives and eighteen children . He died without keeping an inheritance for me and my brothers. I watched my mother struggled to fend for the family until she battled with cancer and slept in the lord in 2014. I was alone facing my world with an unknown future. I had no where to go to and I had no one to help me. I ate junks, sometimes I slept with empty stomach. I will see what I want to buy but I had no money. I had been ridiculed that nothing would come out from my life. It bet with life to become successful no matter how long it would take. While my mother was alive the only world I knew was the world of living to eat and not eating to live. The journey of years of struggle to get out of poverty influenced my decision of making the choice to be rich , comfortable and secure. Most people have their choices to be secure and others rich. It is the choices that you make that will motivate you to desire financial success. It is the choice I made that I would not work hard for money as my father did all his life and died at age 53 in 1995 when he went to collect his pension money leaving my mother with cauldron of problems and nine children to take care of. I rather spend years learning and investing how to make money than work for money. This is the philosophy that guide my life. The tougher the journey the greater the victory and sweeter the story.

MASTER PLAN

The road to financial success begins with a plan. What plan do you have for your financial life? A plan is not about working hard , saving hard and living hard. I had planned since I was 25 to become financial free before I get to 40. It had been a process of self discovery, discipline and mastery. At times when I discover a fault in my plan I change plans quickly or refined them. Things changes and a change can truncate your plan. I have seen people planning to become poor with the way they spend their money and the kind of people they spend their time with. The things you spend your money on and the people you spend time with if it is not productive it is destructive. You association determines your level of elevation. Get my book Great minds think great which I co-authored with Haanyeh Saadat a German based author from Afghanistan. It will help you identify and associate with the right people. If you don't have a master plan for success you will only build castles in the air allowing life to pass through you.

WHAT DO YOU SPEND YOUR MONEY IN?

We all spend money. If we don't spend money the economy suffers. The issue is about how you spend your money and on what you spend your money on? Are you spending money on things that make you rich? Or things that make you poor? Many middle class and poor have a bad money spending habit. They spend without thinking about the possibility of going bankrupt the next day. Their spending rate makes them work harder for money. Give a poor man a million dollar today in the next month he will remain poor because they lack the financial discipline to control and regulate their expenditures. This is what has made many companies and countries bankrupt. Most people spend money on things that will not produce money for you are making yourself poor. If i should buy a book it's a good investment because that book will increase my knowledge and I will always have it with me to read. But if I buy chocolate to lick it is not a productive venture. Except I buy it to sell.

WHAT MONEY CAN BECOME TO YOU?

I don't believe that money is evil. I am not sounding greedy if I say I need more of it. But the way you handle money can become a curse than a blessing. Your money can become an asset to you or a liability. An asset is what makes more money for you and liability takes money from you. You attitude towards money is what it would become.

Money can give you a good sleep and a bad sleep. It determines how you tame it.

WHAT DO YOU WORK FOR?

There are three kinds of income that we all work for both the rich, poor and middle class.

- *Earned Income*
- *Portfolio*
- *Passive Income*

Earned Income: The poor and middle class work for only one kind of income. That is earned income. This is the kind of income that comes from physical labour. People that work for this kind of income work harder and save harder. They have many money problems. Employees and self employed work for this kind of money. If they need more money they look for a higher paying job, get higher qualification and ask for a pay rise through their union.

Portfolio Income: The rich work for paper assets, bonds and stocks. This is called paper money. They accumulate money in paper form.

Passive Income: This is money generating machine of the rich. This is assets that makes the rich richer. The rich earns more money without their money working hard for them through creating and buying assets that makes them richer. If I write a book I have created an asset. I wrote this book to build an estate in Nigeria. It will produce the money for that. You don't need to work for generate a passive income. This is the secret success of the rich.

THE DIFFRENCE IS CLEAR

From the explanation above, you will discover that the rich works for the three basic incomes. Earned income, portfolio and passive income. They are not stereotyped to one source of income. Working for passive income requires a high level of financial intelligence than earned income. That is why only few people become rich by earning passive income than earned income. A change in your thinking to increase you financial intelligence will affects your shift in earning income.

MIND YOUR BUSSINESS

If you want to become rich it's not a fast lane thing. It's a process that you must be prepared to pass through. You can't outsmart the process. Learn to mind your business by taking care of your own business. If you don't mind your own business, you will mind another man's business. I don't advise people to just jump, quit their job and start a business. The business world and employment world are two different worlds. I advise people to learn and upgrade their business skills while working in their spare time and start a small business at home to test their business strength which becomes stronger with time. Building a business is an asset that can make you richer if it has a solid operating system that generates cash flow. Business is different from busyness and cash is different from cash flow.

WHO GETS KILLED?

I have seen people after attending a seminar or reading a great book get motivated to start a business. They pump money into the business, furnish an office , employ workers , run adverts and promotions to attract customers to kill big with their products and services after few months they cannon gun bounces back and they are the ones that finally get killed out of business.

DEPENDENCE VS INDEPENDENCE

Many people have been programmed right from childhood by their parents for dependence before handling them over to teachers who do a perfect job by making them over dependent on them for success and later release them to their employers , bosses and government to take care of them till their working days is over. If you want to depend on the government , company and family for your financial security you can stop reading this book right on this page. Bur if you want to take charge of your financial future by been independent you can proceed the remaining part of this book is for you.

CRITICAL THINKING

We humans are higher thinking creatures. But they way most people think you will wonder if they are really humans or animals. Who does your thinking? Do you do you thinking or your teachers, employers and companies help you do you thinking about what you want to achieve in life. Most people are in financial trouble today because of the opinion they accepted from people. Our economic problem as a nation can be traced from the incompetent people that think for us as a nation which affects us all. You should be able to think and plan for your financial future. Refuse to accept what any boy thinks or tell you. During my trials years I was advised by family and friends to get a job and stop wasting my time. I objected their advise and forged ahead with my life.

ENVISION YOUR FUTURE

You should have a glue about your vision and see where you want to be and what you want to achieve from now till the next five, ten years. The future to enjoy the fruits of your labour begins today not tomorrow. Winners take up the challenges today, while failures run away waiting to face their challenges another day. Today is the future not tomorrow. Show me a looser and I will tell you a man that refuse to fight today. You can have anything you want in life if you will be willing to take action to fight today.

SURVIVING TODAYS WORLD

What you know yesterday can be irrelevant today. Before our very eyes things that we use to know today have been rendered obsolete. Old rules and ideas of money of yester years can't work for you in today's flexible world. You need to be opened to information and continuous upgrading your financial intelligence by sharpening your saw. People that are struggling today are the people that have been left behind who are still operating with the old rules of money which is work hard and save money.

KEY POINTS

- ✓ Most people spend money on things that will not produce money for you are making yourself poor.
- ✓ You attitude towards money is what it would become.
- ✓ A change in your thinking to increase you financial intelligence will affects your shift in earning income.

- ✓ If you don't mind your own business, you will mind another man's business.
- ✓ Most people are in financial trouble today because of the opinion they accepted from people.
- ✓ You can have anything you want in life if you will be willing to take action to fight today.
- ✓ People that are struggling today are the people that have been left behind who are still operating with the old rules of money which is work hard and save money.

PART FOUR

MONEY MASTERY

"There is only one way to get anybody to do anything, and that is by making the other person want to do it."
- Dale Carnegie

JUST A TIP OF THE ICE BERGE

You are about to learn what the rich know and practice which they will never share with you. View this chapter as a crystal ball that will unveil the secrets of attaining financial success. Don't be in haste to read through, read to understand and take notes if you don't mind. By the time you finish this chapter you will discover why you shouldn't bother working hard for money any longer. But your money working harder for you.

SUCCESS MADE EASY

Achieving success can be easy depending on the process you want to take. The school only taught us that there is only one way of doing things and only one answer for questions. But in the real cruel world people that adapt to such rules don't survive. There are many ways of doing things and different answers to questions if you must get to the top. There are many ways to become financial independent and get rich without much struggle once you discover the formula and later initiate your formula for success.

BEYOUND READING

I have heard authors and speakers tell people to read business and self help books it will make them rich. That is fallacy. If you don't practice the principles in this book your life would remain the same. Practice makes the magic. I don't only write for profit motive but to see lives been transformed. I have seen people that read thousands of books their lives are still how they had been. They have only acquired knowledge but lack the power to bring it to physical equivalent.

EXPERINECE IS THE BEST TEACHER

I spent years in school and graduated without been thought how to make money. I knew that I wouldn't be a loyal employee because I don't like doing what people like. I want to think for my self and do things in my own way. I had great opportunities of having the right people, excess cash but I lack experience and financial intelligence to make money. My first business was an entertainment business that lasted for just a week and closed. I wanted to become a reggae musician. My late mother believed in my dream and gave 50,000NGN to invest in my music career. I traveled down to Lagos Nigeria to pursue my musical dream with high hopes and ambition for success. While in Lagos I met an event manager who advised me and to invest to stage up a concert to make money for my self. I had no experience in show business I pumped my money into the project. Luck shined on me as an unpopular upcoming artiste I pulled crowd to the event, tickets was sold with tight security. While I was performing on stage, my money was been divided at the gate and stolen away by the event manager. I was left stranded and penniless. The next day I was out of business.

After few months of struggling to survive doing menial jobs I met a friend and we started a movie company where we admit and train young actors to participate in our

TV and movie productions. I was privileged to partner with Angels media a company that has good movie equipments. I had about 200 casts, registrations was good and I was back into business. I had all the support I needed from my casts and people but I lack experience and financial intelligence. A project took me three years to produce. It was later abandoned. I had good productions but I lack the skill to make it profitable. I looked smart and intelligent but I was incompetent and my incompetence led to the demise of the business. If what I knew today about making money I had knew in those years I would have been a millionaire. Ignorance is a disease. An ignorant person is proud and not willing to learn anything new. I paid for my foolishness with long years of suffering.

But my long years of suffering and mediocrity opened me to a new direction in life. Which I am happy about today.

BE PREPARED

Making money is about increasing your financial intelligence. You must have a flexible minds that is willing to learn. People that brag a lot have nothing upstairs. The only brag to hide their deficiencies. Making money requires investing your life, money , time and energy to acquire financial knowledge. How would you want to become rich and not be prepared to invest in your financial education? The greatest investment that you can make before you become rich is to invest in your financial education. You will learn what the school deprived you learning and made you a working slave for money. Your mental shift is about to change as you are about to learn what will change your financial future.

MENTAL SHIFT

It's a gradual process to transform your self a money working machine to having a money making machine. Employees are programmed to work like slaves in the plantation. To shift from the mindset of an employee to a business owner and investor requires a change in mind set and philosophy. Employee are trained to work for money and business owners are made to employ employees to make money and their money also work hard for them through their assets.

SOMETHING FOR NOTHING

Most people want to become rich through the easiest means possible. The want to make quick money. Over night success I knew from personal experience doesn't exist if it had existed for someone else. People want to get something for nothing without effort. Making money still requires your effort. Thomas Jefferson advised that; " The worst day of a man's life is when he sits down and begins thinking about how he can get something for nothing." There is an emotional , economic sociological epidemic sweeping across the world. Destroying individuals and threatening the future of civilization. It is a disease like cancer that makes people unable to function normally. Brain Tracy addresses it as mental illness. You can't become rich and escape poverty with something for nothing. You must have smoothing for something. You must have something valuable to sell to attract money.

WE ALL HAVE SOMETHING TO SELL

There is no any other way to become rich without providing a valuable service or product in exchange for money. As long as we are breathing we have something that some needs. In the first period of my writing career I wrote many books that never sold well in the international market. I never gave up because the right person haven't read my book and the world are yet to realize how useful and powerful the principles in my books can do. As long as I am into writing there are people who are reading my books and its is influencing their lives positively and they are enriching me. You must have something that people must be willing to pay for . We are all into selling in one way or the other. Babies sell when they cry demanding for breast milk from their mother. If you want to be rich you should have something to sell to a large number of people. Zig Ziglar philosophy states that; " If you can help as many people get everything they want that is the secret of success." I struggled financially for years because I was intelligent and creative but not entrepreneurial. I wrote good books but I couldn't sell them, I produced good films and music I couldn't sell them. Because of fear of rejection.

OVER COMING MY FEAR

I knew I was alone, I had no one who can help me overcome my fear of selling. I never knew I had great potentials in selling until after I failed and tried. I look for market to sell my service as a motivational speaker by writing proposals to schools and churches. Some call me and some don't. I wrote my story books for my company creative pen embassy and sold them my self to schools. I was using it as a leverage to sharpen my sales skill. Many people thought that I was jobless they never knew I was undergoing a great life education. I had great books on amazon.com yet I was always promoting my books on social media drawing traffic to my e-store. It took me years to develop and maximize my sales skill. Robert Kiyosaki one of my great teacher and mentor said; "*I am not a best writing author but I am a best selling author.*" I agree with him. I can sell anything an idea, a product and service. If I had not overcome the fear of rejection I would have never become successful in life. If you want to make money you must learn how to sell your idea to the world. Poor sales skill make companies go bankrupt. When you stop earning your business stops growing. I devoted my life to sales seminar, training and reading great books on sales. I practiced while no one was watching in my cooperation not someone's else cooperation. Pick the book and the teacher will appear.

DO THE WORK

You must work towards becoming financial free. People who are lazy prefer to look for safety nets of job security where they would be receiving wages and salaries monthly. If you don't invest your time to do the work nothing will happen. No one can do it for you. You are meant to carry your cross alone till you get to the top. I have seen people invest their money without dedicating their time to learn how to invest. If you don't dedicate your time to learn how to swim the day you will attempt to swim be prepared to get drowned. That is how many people are. They want to become rich but they are not willing to pay the price to get rich. Everybody want to go to heaven but nobody wants to die.

SCHOOL OF MONEY

While the poor and middle class value academic and professional education. The rich values financial education. Academic and professional education has limitation to make you wealthy. Education to the rich is not an event but a way of life. Financial education is a life long learning. The school of money is the school of the rich. If you want to be rich you must attend the school of money. It is in these school that millionaires and billionaires are made. You can't see a rich person who is not a compulsory learner and reader of financial intelligence , wealth creation, accumulation , investment and self improvement books. I have heard people say without academic education someone can't become successful in life. That statement is for people that accept it to be true and become a reality. If you want to be rich what you need is to attend the school of money to increase your financial intelligence.

SMART PEOPLE

The world place highly academic and professional people to be the smartest people in life. I have heard and seen these so called smart people brag about their academic qualifications and grades. If they are really smart why are they looking for jobs and clinging to jobs? Why are they working for money all their lives? They brag and argue about their academic achievements when they have nothing to show. They day the stop working is the day they start dying.   How smart are they?

WORK FOR FREE

Can you really work for free without receiving a pay check? Working for free means working without money. If you can work for free you will be conditioned to never work for money. You will have more time for yourself to learn and study more to increase your financial intelligence and gain real world business experience. Most people think working for free is a stupid thing to do. But that is the best thing to do. I have never worked for money or applied for a job. I go into partnership or join a company to just upgrade my skills and increase my knowledge. People who work free get richer than people who work hard for money. Working for money will condition you to become a slave to money. Working for free will condition you to be master over your life, time and money.

EXPAND YOUR CONTEXT

Don't limit the size of your context through your thinking. Expand your context for the possibility to become rich and financial free. Many people who struggle spending their years working hard for money find it hard to expand their context. They have many reasons and excuses why they need to keep working. They prefer physical hard work than mental hard work. They stick to their limited context instead of increasing the financial content in their brain.

ACT LIKE A WINNER

The attitude of winning the race to financial freedom is by expanding the content in your context. You winning attitude would make you change bad luck into good luck, failure into success and mediocrity into excellence. Winners don't look at bad conditions before stepping out. They are prepared for the best and worst conditions that life throws on their path. Winners keep an open mind towards success no matter the circumstances they find themselves. They always have the possibility of winning than losing. They are radical risk takers that can go extra mile to achieve what they want because of their scope of reality wrapped in unlimited possibilities.

LOSSERS PLIGHT

Losers are afraid of facing challenges. They want the easiest means in life with secured guarantee. People looking for guarantee jobs, and paychecks are real losers. They want things to go their own way. Their reality is wrapped with guarantee than possibilities. They know they can never win even if they try. Because they have losers content in their context.

FIGHTING SPIRIT

It takes a fighting spirit to change and stick to your reality. People will look for ways to discourage you when they don't see immediate evidence of what you do. If your spirit is weak they can change your reality and if it is strong they can't. Seeing my father struggled financially and my family I have vowed never to work for money all my life but learn how money can work for me. Friends, girl friends and family members thought I am out of my mind. Because we have different realities. Instead of making someone richer, I rather make my self richer. I stuck to my reality facing the world with just my dreams striving into a great future which I have envisioned in my mind eye.

EMOTIONAL INTELLIGENCE

Most of the times our emotions stop us from doing some kind of things. Mastering our emotion is a great advantage. Most people that look for the easiest means to get rich lack the emotional control to face difficulties.

When challenges raises its ugly head they take flight instead of fight. Lack of financial discipline is a product of emotional intelligence. Most people cant wait to satisfy their immediate gratification. Helen Keller said; " True happiness is not found in immediate gratification but in the fulfillment of one's calling through purpose." If you can control your emotion you can control your money and increase your financial intelligence.

SUNDAY SCHOOL LESSON

Nobody was created by God to be a slave. In the story of creation I was taught in Sunday school that God created man and woman and blessed them to dominate the air, rivers and land and multiply. Many people have become slaves to money that they should dominate and multiply. Instead of making themselves richer, they are making other people richer by working hard for them. This words of to dominate and multiply has guided my steps in life and changed my reality for success.

LEARN FROM YOUR ANCESTORS

More than 100 years ago our ancestors were independent entrepreneurs. They were farmers, traders, hunters, black smith and craft men. The idea of job came in during the industrial age when cooperation, industries needed workers to work. A good education, high pay and benefits was guaranteed. This turned our parents into employees and laborers. Thereby abolishing the reality of our ancestors as entrepreneurs. Our parents adopted a new reality of job security and passed the same reality to their children telling them to go to school, get good grades and get a high paying job.

THE BERLIN WALLS

In 1989 the Berlin walls brought down the industrial age when the world wide web was born ushering us into the information age. Which officially ended in 2000. This shift created more opportunities for young entrepreneur millionaires through the web.

The world we are in is a world of entrepreneurship, a capitalist society where been uneducated, unskilled is not a criteria for success. You can become rich from where ever you are starting with nothing to become something.

KEY POINTS

✓ The school only taught us that there is only one way of doing things and only one answer for questions.

✓ If you don't practice the principles in this book your life would remain the same.

✓ The greatest investment that you can make before you become rich is to invest in your financial education.

✓ This words of to dominate and multiply has guided my steps in life and changed my reality for success.

✓ You can't become rich and escape poverty with something for nothing.

PART FIVE

FINANCIAL EDUCATION

"All of life is action and passion, and not to be involved in the action and passions of your time is to run the risk of not having truly lived."
- Plotinus

CHOOSE YOUR PATH

E = Employee

S = Self Employed

B = Business owner

I = Investor

EMPLOYEES: Work hard for money and help other people get richer all their lives. The day the stop working they stop receiving money.

SELF EMPLOYED: The do things themselves , working for themselves. The day the stop working is the day they stop making money.

BUSSINESS OWNER: This are the people that play the game of the rich. The richest people fall in this category. They build business, employ smart employees to work for them and invest in other assets that generate cash flow. Their business and assets work hard for them.

INVESTOR: These are people with excess money looking for business owners to invest their money into their business to make their money work hard for them.

TAKE THIS SERRIOUSLY

Working hard for money won't make you rich. Working for someone only makes the person rich not you. Instead of working for money and making another person rich why don't you learn how you can make yourself richer?

If you want to become rich you must become self employed that is learn to work for yourself and grow into a business owner and investors. Start small but don't stay small. That is the problem with been self employed. Many people feel trapped been self employed because they don't trust people working with them and they can't manage people. They produce and market their products and services themselves. It's hard to expand into a big business. Business owner needs people to work for them. They need good team of smart employees who will work for them and make money for them. Investors need smart competent business people to multiply their money for them. Their money work hard for them.

CHOOSING MY PATH

My family background helped to spur my decision of choosing my career path in life. My father was an educated and dedicated employee rising to the rank of a supervisor with NRC Nigerian Railway Cooperation. He worked hard for the government and money all his life. After retirement he became self employed as a cab driver with his car. He couldn't survive the business world because he lacked the business skills and experience to survive all by himself without a pay check. He was hardly paid pension, he struggled with bad health and poverty till his death. He died in the process of trying to go and collect the pension money he has worked for all his life in the year 1995. I grew up to watch my family struggle financially and I hated job security. Because, I realized from an early stage in life that there is no security found in job security after my father was thrown out of the job he taught would protect him when his working days were over. He found himself in a cruel world where making money was challenging for him.

My mother had been a business woman with chains of small business in form of a restaurant, electric store, grocery store and hair dressing saloon. These business was managed by her children which many of them used to train themselves to school. She supported my father when things where rough for him. She covered his nakedness without making people realize the frustration he was in. She was independent and not dependent on any of her children or the government to take care of her as my father did. She was able to send her children abroad and established business that still thrived today inherited by her children. While my father left none but antiquity properties. I don't mean to sound arrogant but I am trying to make a point.

While in school I never allowed my mind set to be programmed to go and work as an employee. I had made up my mind to follow my mother's foot step of becoming an entrepreneur and a business owner. I wanted to make money by my money working hard for me without me working for money all my life like my father did. This decision is what has led me this far in life. I have family members that believe so much in their academic qualification like my father did and they refused to increase their financial intelligence or start a business in their spare time. Most of them are out of job will some are still clinging to jobs. We all have difference in our reality that is why they accuse me of dreaming and thinking about big things that I cannot achieve based on the limitation of the content in their context.

LET'S TALK ABOUT MONEY

Many people consider talking about money as evil . Talking about money is not evil. To my best of understanding is the process of acquiring the money that is evil. If you decide to work hard for money without stealing it its your hard earned money it's not evil. If my money works hard for me and I became rich why should I say its evil? Many families and religions forbid their children from talking about money. When you don't like talking about money how can you become rich. Talking about money is an opportunity for us to learn how to make money or work for money depending on your choice. There is nothing evil in talking about money, investments, business and success. Just as we enjoy talking about sex, sport and politics why don't we love to talk about money? It is by talking that we get to discover and learn something's that we never knew about life. If you want to work for money all your life and you don't want to talk about it is suicidal.

THE BIGGEST LIES

The biggest liars will say " I don't need money" " I don't want to be rich" " I am comfortable with my life." These are big lies people tell themselves. As long as we are alive we all need money. The people that say all these things need money more than us that really need it. Living in denial id dangerous, whatever you think and say to yourself becomes a reality . Words are powerful. What you say and wish for your self becomes part of you. People who lie that they don't need money are always living a life of needy and living without money. "Only the truth shall set you free "If you tell yourself you shall be free financially and enjoy the abundance riches that money can offer.

MIND SET OF THE ENTRAPRENEUR

Entrepreneurs think and act differently. They are selfless and willing to serve more people by helping them solve their problems through providing valuable products and services. Entrepreneurs see opportunities and capitalizes on them not problems that people see and complain about. Entrepreneurs turn disadvantages into advantages. They don't see opportunities and keep it to themselves to profit from it alone. The set up a team to execute the opportunity and maximize profit. An entrepreneur know how to raise money from investors and work with business owners to leverage their products and services. If you see an opportunity and keep it to yourself and later take advantage of it you are a small business person or self employed. Why some small business and self employed remain small is because they can solve problems they can solve. They don't need people to help them solve problems.

WHAT IS YOUR MONEY DOING FOR YOU?

Many people have been programmed like robots to work harder than their money and spend to satisfy their immediate gratification. They were never taught how their money can work for them. Because their teachers also work hard for money. A duck can't teach a pig how to sing. What they think is investing is pilling their money in their savings account or retirement account as they continue to work harder.

Ignorantly while they work harder, they think that their money is also working harder for them. This is financial ignorance and illiteracy.

FINANCIAL IGNORANCE

Financial ignorance is disease of the mind. This seventh quality of human nature is inevitable and unavoidable. Socrates the great philosopher admitted that he is unintelligent and ignorant despite his vast knowledge. Confucius never dazzled anyone with his super knowledge. No matter how smart or well educated you are it is impossible for you to know everything. You could be a smart educated financial advisor on wall street. Yet within twenty four hours, thousands of the facts and figures reflected in stock prizes and market activities will change. What you think is right today could be wrong the next day. The word perfect knowledge doesn't exist. The amount you know about anything is tiny compared to the vast amount you do not know. For this reason, no matter how intelligent or educated , everyone is ignorant to some degree.

CONTINEOUS LEARNING

If you continue learn to upgrade your skill and level of knowledge, continually have experiences and learn from them you will have fewer mistakes than you had made in the beginning. People who think that they are smarter than everyone and boast about their academic knowledge as a guarantee for success are the dumbest people. Their pride will not make them learn. Their arrogance blocks their mind from accepting new ideas. A university professor can become a financial imbecile. If ignorance blinds your reality you will end up a victim of poverty. The smartest people are willing to open their mind to learn and know more and accept they know nothing.

MORE FACTS ABOUT MAKING MONEY

To think that it takes money to make money is a product of financial ignorance. It depends on the knowledge of who is having the money. It takes financial intelligence and high financial literacy to make money with little effort.

THE FAIRY TALE

My problem with the school system is that they are producing more poor people than rich people giving them fairy tales that competing for grades in the class room and throwing them to compete in the labour market is the best way to make them rich , secure and comfortable in life. Many people leave school programmed with this mindset that is the reason why the want to work hard for money, spend and save money to buy a home and a car. At a point in their live when the pay check stops coming and the benefits they will begin to face the real world realizing that they had wasted their productive live enriching the government and their companies without enriching themselves. At this point in time they would want start their life all over again from scratch just as my father did but he couldn't survive the pressure. The fairy tale of job security forever is over . People that cling to job security and benefits are living a life full with fairy tales.

WHAT ARE YOU WORKING FOR?

For every action there is a reaction. We all have our reasons for working to make money, get out of debt, save and become financial free. If these are your reasons good luck to you. Are you working to become richer or poorer> Many people are working to make themselves poorer than becoming richer. I am not saying that you should quit your job. In my new book Mind your business I taught people how they can quit their job and start their own business from a simple idea and grow into a big business. With other small home based business that they can do to start learning the business skill while still working.

WHAT MAKES THE RICH RICHER

What makes the rich richer more than the middle class and the poor is that the rich build assets that produces cash flow for them without physical effort. The poor and middle class work harder, longer and charge more money acquiring liabilities that make them struggle financially for a steady pay check through their expenses.

ASSETS

Assets makes the rich richer. With an asset you don't need to work hard. It makes your money work harder for you to become richer. There are many types of assets that can make you rich. Assets generates passive income, it is a channel that floods money into your pocket with ease.

RICH

ASSETS	LIABILITY
Real Estates Business Portfolio Products / commodities	

POOR

ASSETS	LIABILITIES
Job	Expenses

The rich have no liabilities but more assets . The poor and middle class asset is their job which produces income which turns into liabilities through expenses.

If you spend more than you earn your business and job can become a liability than an asset.

WHAT INCOME DO YOU WORK FOR?

Many people are working hard for an unknown income. What matters to them is the pay check. If you don't know what type of income you work for you will struggle working hard all your life time and never realize it. I stated earlier in this book that there are three kinds of income. They are:

1. Earned income
2. Portfolio
3. Passive income

There are other kinds of income. Most people go to school to get good grades to work for earned income. If you want to become rich you must have knowledge about other kinds of income. Some of the other incomes are:

4. Residual income: This form of income comes from a business, net working business or a franchise business which you own but someone else runs it for you.

5. Dividend income: This can be income from stocks.
6. Interest income: This is income that comes from savings or bonds.
7. Royalty income: This is a form of income that comes from intellectual properties, books, songs, movies you have written and produced , trademarks and patents.
8. Financial instrument: This income comes from trust deeds from real estate.

   You need to research and study how you can make money from all these types of income if you don't want to work hard for money all your life and exhaust energy doing hard labour.

EDUCATION IS EXPENSIVE

If you think education is expensive try ignorance. It took me years to pay for my ignorance. Many people don't want to invest their time and life to gain knowledge. Education is expensive, attending seminars is expensive it's not what everyone can afford. Going to study business management and entrepreneurship in the university is expensive. Instead of teaching you how to make money, they teach you how to go and work for money. I feel that people should have the privileged to get educated at a nominal fee that is why I write books that will improve their life and increase their financial well-being. Financial and motivational education is my brand of education to help people become richer and happier in life.

DO YOU BELIEVE?

Believe is a strong weapon. What you believe in becomes a reality that sharpens your life. Your believe reflects in the mirror of life. Do you believe that you can stop working hard for money and make your money work harder for you? Do you believe that saving money is the riskiest thing to do? Do you believe that you can earn more with less. These are the believes that will change your financial future. If you don't believe this reality there can't be possibility for achieving financial independence in your life. These are the believes that can change your reality and produce solutions to solve your financial problems.

GET YOUR MONEY BACK GURANTEE

If after reading this book you don't find anything meaningful. You can return the book and get your money back. Since you are reading this book and actively increasing your financial intelligence you are on the right track you can read further. Your greatest asset is your financial IQ keep investing in your financial education.

PART SIX

ALCHEMY OF WEALTH

"Whenever you see a successful business, someone once made a courageous decision."
- **Peter Drucker**

-

MORDERN ALCHEMIST

In the 18th century alchemist were known to transform dust into gold with the philosopher stone. In this 21st century the world is filled with few modern days alchemist who can create something from nothing. The mind is the philosopher stone that you can use to make the impossible to become possible. I faced the world with nothing when starting out. Everything that I have accomplished began with just an idea into a valuable product and service which has produced millions for me. Many people allow lack of money to stop them. They believe that nothing can be achieved without money that is why they remain where they are waiting for the moon to come to them.

THREAT TO BILLIONIARES

Everyday young hungry minded entrepreneurs are emerging from different parts of the world starting with nothing to hit the million dollar mark and breaking through the rank of billionaires through the internet. They are competing like birds in the sky with super rich.

Location is no longer a barrier as long as you know what you are doing you can become rich where ever you are if you have the mindset of a modern day alchemist.

MY ANSWER TO A CLERGY

On as Sunday morning I attended a church service in Lagos, Nigeria. The pastor of the church asked a simple question to his congregation saying; " Can anyone live without money?" Everybody said " No" I was the only one that said "Yes" and he asked me to explain why I disagreed with what everybody said. I told him that if we learn to live with money we would want to work for money all our lives. But if we think we don't need money to survive we would be focused, purpose driven and motivated to make our money work for us. He laughed and told me that without money nothing can be achieved and he quoted a biblical verse which states; " Money answereth all things." He is a pastor and a university lecturer who works for money so he just expressed his reality and defended it.

MONEY IN MY MIND

I am not encouraging any one to do this based on our different realities in life. We all know our strength and weakness. If you want to become richer faster you need to change your reality by believing that you can live without money. If you believe that without money you can't survive you will continue to be a slave to money and it will control your life and destiny. I might look broke and penniless but deep in my mind is a money printing machine that is printing out millions of ideas to be converted into physical cash.

QUITTERS RARELY WIN

Sometimes I would go to bed with hungry stomach, I might fall ill, I have bills to pay. I never felt discouraged to give up and go and get a job to earn pay check. I would focus on my goal by generating solutions to solve my financial problems. I will envision my future picture and my net worth and I will be filled with enthusiasm to rise above my challenges.

GO GET A JOB

I have been advised by families and friends to go and get a job. Preferable a teaching job by the people who think they care about me. Which I know they don't because of the difference in our reality. I have been against the way teachers are used by the government as agents that produce wage slaves for the government and train students to go and work hard for money instead of helping them discover and maximize their potentials. The problem we are economic crisis we experiencing today was contributed by the schools. They did a perfect job for the government by producing people who will depend on the government for their well-being instead of been trained to be independent. There is no need to explain why I don't need a job for people that love the coffers of job security.

CHANGE THE WORLD

I am not the messiah. I can't change the world and you can't change the world. We just have to change our world. Which begins with a change of our mindset, mentality and realities about success, money and life. If I hadn't changed my reality to increase my financial intelligence I wouldn't have written this book that will help you increase your financial intelligence. I have helped to change my world by advocating financial literacy and motivation for the total well-being of humanity. Mahatma Gandhi said; " Be the change you want the world to see." That begins with unveiling your reality to the world.

APOLOGY TO MY EMPLOYEE FRIENDS

A friend of mine was giving me ride down town. And I was showing a lady in the car some of my books on the internet. She was excited after reading the summary of Naira Crisis. She asked me what motivated me to write the book? And I told her that I wrote the book to help any one that is tired of been a wage slave and wants to improve their life by increasing their financial intelligence. My friend driving took it personal and he began accusing me insulting employees that it is not every one that is meant to become an entrepreneur that it's a risky thing to do. He wouldn't advise anyone to quit his job to become an entrepreneur. I still repeated what I told the lady that my book is not for everyone but for anyone that is tired of been a wage slave and wants to improve their life by increasing their financial intelligence. He used the word risky. He can't bear the risk even though he claims to also be an entrepreneur since he sell products and work as an employee.

ITS YOUR JOB TO GET RICH NOT YOUR BOSS

Many people have the mentality that working hard for their boss is the right thing to do. They think that is the easiest route to riches. They are only working hard to make their boss richer and they get poorer. They reality is that; they are blind folded by paychecks to realize the truth. Your boss and company doesn't make you rich but exploit you. Your boss job is to make sure you are well paid for your hard work. Therefore, it is your job to make yourself rich. Instead of me to teach in another person's school I would rather start my own school. Instead of me to look for a movie to act to be paid for my talent; I would rather produce my movie. The path to creating your fortune and attaining freedom is by becoming your own boss. You are the captain of your fate and master of your life.

FINDING PASSION

Passion is doing what you love. I have never seen someone that excel in doing what they don't love. Doing what you love is the secret to success. Passion is the key that unlocks opportunities and maximize potentials. I wrote a book titled ; Passion is the key it's a book that will help you transform what you love into wealth. The great richest people on earth are people that succeeded doing what they love not what people want them to love. The content in the book will expose you to discovering your life task and living on purpose. You can order for it on amazon.com. Many people are worried about how they can earn a living. You don't need to worry anymore just find your passion and success will begin to open doors of opportunities to you. I have passion for writing, speaking and teaching and I build a career out of it as an author, speaker and educator. Many people are frustrated doing jobs that they don't like and they don't want to quit to find a job that aligns with their passion. Dele

Carnegie asserted; "Show me a man who is passionate for what he does and I would tell you his entire philosophy." People who are interested in paychecks never find their passion.

BEEN RICH IS NOT ENOUGH

Been rich is not enough you need to expand your context and reality. Many rich people still work for money just to maintain their status quo. We have rich athletes, actors and artistes that still work for money. When they stop working for some time they would soon get broke and running into debts. You need to think about creating lasting wealth. Being wealthy means surviving for years without physical work and still maintaining a good standard of living. And after death there is abundance of wealth left to be inherited by your immediate family. Many rich people die with their riches. True freedom comes from accumulating wealth than riches.

PATH TO FREEDOM

Choose your path to financial freedom through job security, financial security and financial freedom.

JOB SECURITY

I am not trying to belittle employees who prefer job security. Life is a matter of choice. If you feel you lack the courage and emotional intelligence to survive in the real world. You can stick to what you know and do the best you can. Most people that cling to job security assume that it meant financial security. There is really no security found in job security until you get to laid off or retired. You need to think out of the box and go beyond job security. This is the hardest path to attain financial freedom.

FINANCIAL SECURITY

Financial security comes from increasing your financial intelligence and creating assets that will keep multiplying your money weather you work or not. Instead of working hard invest in assets not liabilities.

FINANCIAL FREEDOM

Financial freedom comes from your money and people working hard for you. You have freedom to work or not to work. This is where your financial knowledge and business skills pays off. This is the greater path that will give you guaranteed security, wealth and independence for life.

MONEY AND FREEDOM

I have met many people with millions pilled in their bank accounts with high paying jobs and business. They invest their money in investments they know nothing about. If that investment fails, their job ends and their business disappears they will be wiped out without their trace been seen.

WHEN THE WIND BLOWS

There will always be economic upheaval there is always transfer of wealth. Opportunities are created and more problems are created. It has no respect weather you have money or not. You just need to be prepared to invest and keep increasing your financial intelligence not to be blown away by the economic wind. Crisis makes heroes and casualties. Be prepared for good and worst times.

KEY POINTS

- ✓ The mind is the philosopher stone that you can use to make the impossible to become possible.
- ✓ Location is no longer a barrier as long as you know what you are doing you can become rich where ever you are if you have the mindset of a modern day alchemist.
- ✓ if we learn to live with money we would want to work for money all our lives. But if we think we don't need money to survive we would be focused, purpose driven and motivated to make our money work for us.
- ✓ The path to creating your fortune and attaining freedom is by becoming your own boss. You are the captain of your fate and master of your life.
- ✓ You don't need to worry anymore just find your passion and success will begin to open doors of opportunities to you.
- ✓ Being wealthy means surviving for years without physical work and still maintaining a good standard of living. And after death there

is abundance of wealth left to be inherited by your immediate family.

✓ You just need to be prepared to invest and keep increasing your financial intelligence not to be blown away by the economic wind.

PART SEVEN
MONEY MACHINE
CASH FLOW

" There are powers inside of you, which, if you could discover and use, would make of you everything you ever dreamed or imagined you could become."

- Orson Swett Marden

THE GAME OF MONEY

We all play the game of money as long as we want to make money. The middle class and the poor play the game of money working hard for money. The rich plays the game of money differently. If you want to beat the rich, you must learn, study and master these game of money called cash flow. Cash flow is the product of an excellent financial intelligence. This is your mastery over your money. It's the power that you have to control your cash.

CASH TO THRASH

Many people that work for money turn their cash into thrash because of their poor money management skill. People spend money on things that make them poor and force them to work harder because of the fear of going out of money. Their cash becomes a thrash of liabilities to their lives . The rich turn thrash into cash making more cash. The potential power of financial knowledge empowers you with the skill to turn thrash into cash.

MONEY PROBLEMS

The reason why many people struggle financially is that they believe that simple making more money will solve our financial problems. It causes more bigger problems than solve their problems. Most people will continue to suffer financial problems because they lack financial management skills. Most people know how to write, calculate, memorize , read to pass and compete for grades. They are trained to solve mathematical problems but not solve financial problems. They were only trained to believe working hard for money is the answer to solve their financial problems. That is financial illiteracy. Cash flow mismanagement is the cause of their financial problem.

MONOPOLY

The rich are the masters of monopoly. They are in control of their money. They control how much income flows in and expenses that flows out of their pocket. A good cash flow management is the process when more flows in than flows out of your pocket. The power of monopoly is your ability to control your money directly without external interference. Monopoly makes the rich smarter and richer. If you don't make more money flowing in from your assets you will struggle to become rich and if the cash keeps flowing out through expenses with little flowing in you will suffer financial cancer. Having more cash without control makes people poorer making them spend more and go into debt. You need a financial statement to be able to checkmate and monitor your level of income and expenses. This is the play book of the rich.

FINANCIAL STATEMENT

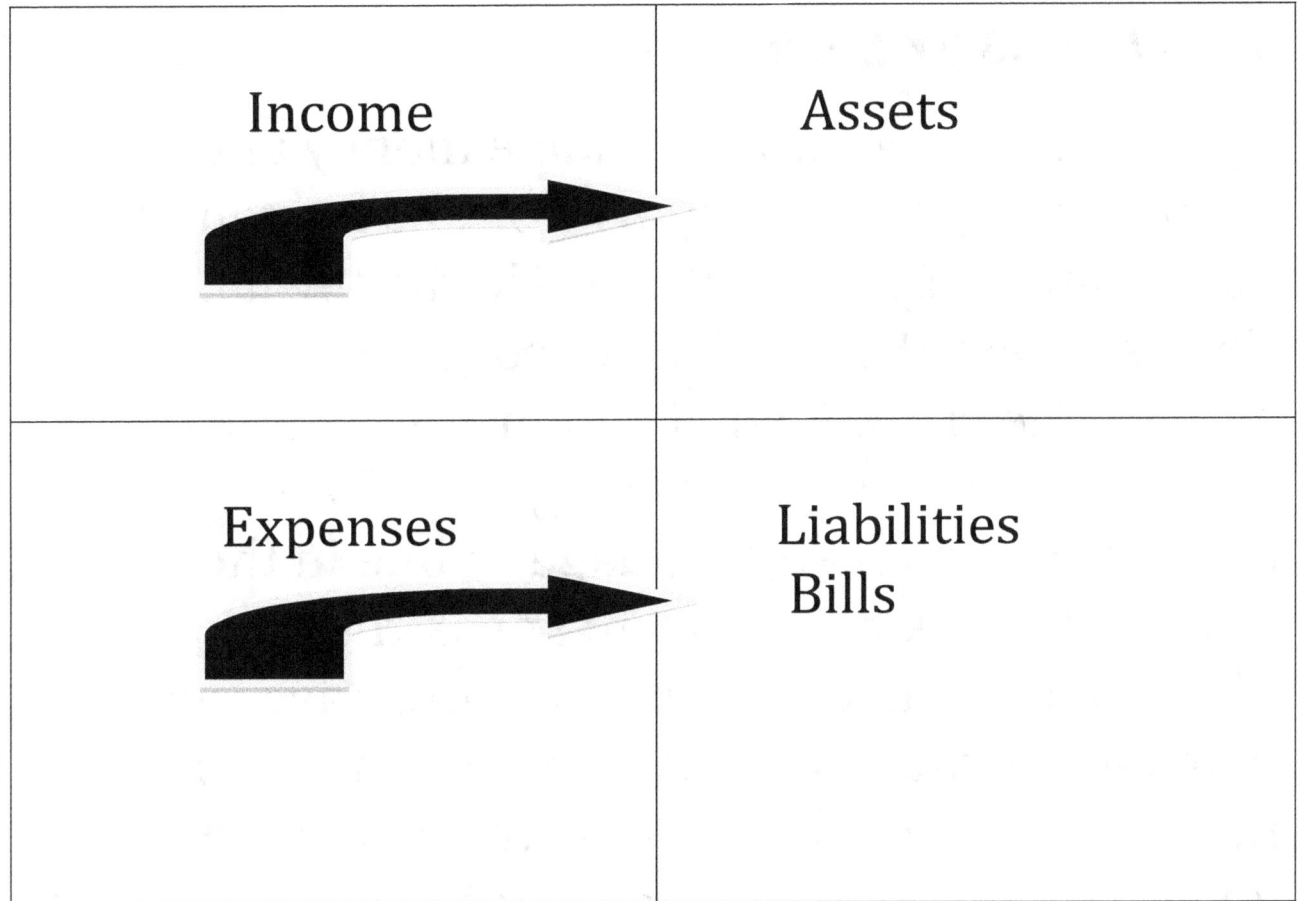

Income	Assets
Expenses	Liabilities Bills

When most people always have bills to pay daily, weekly and monthly especially earned income people. They cannot get ahead financially. If you can control your cash flow you will keep making someone richer and helping someone control your money into their pockets. Think for a moment are you making someone richer and making yourself poorer? You need to learn this basic financial theory to increase your financial literacy.

SPEAK MONEY LANGUAGE

Many people want to make money and they keep working for money without having an idea about how to speak and write in money language. This is where the rich has an edge over the poor and middle class. To make money you must understand and speak its language. Every profession has their language. While in the university is learned how to speak the language of the theatre. Lawyers and doctors have their language , principles and terminologies. You need to be able to know how to read money language in form of financial statement and write money language in figures. Your ability to read figures will make you financially intelligent.

POWER OF LEVERAGE

Leverage in a simple term is doing more , achieving more and doing more with less. Putting cash in the bank is not a leverage. But taking away money from the bank is a form of leverage.

Saving is a game of losers who don't know what to do with their money so their bank help them to take very good care of it. Investment is the game of winners who know how to multiply their money. If the power of leverage is not properly used it would be abused. It becomes risky when you don't have financial intelligence and you want to invest in something you can't control. Leveraging is what makes the rich get richer and work smarter with less or little effort. You can leverage on peoples time and money. If you want to be rich quickly don't depend on your earned income or capital gains. You must depend and use other peoples, time, money and resources to achieve what you want. The internet is a good form of leverage for me. I don't need to travel far to do business, search for markets and publishing companies to publish my books. All I have to do is to write a book like this send it a publishing company and in few days my book is published and made ready for sale on amazon.com, Lulu.com, Konga.com and blurb.com and people will start placing orders. These companies are responsible for the shipping world wide without my effort and resources. The social media is a system is leverage on to advertise, promote and keep relationship with my books readers and clients. I can be in a room with the internet I am global. Most people have laptops, IPods and smart phones they don't know what to do with them. It is not about having all these gadgets that counts but how well do you leverage on it.

DEBT NOT DEATH

Many people think that debt is bad. If a debt is used properly and generates profit it's a good debt. And if it is not properly used it is bad debt. A good used debt is a good debt that makes you richer and a bad debt is a trap of death. Through debt the rich leverage on other people's money to invest to get richer. While, the poor and middle class get entrapped into the trap of death based on their poor financial intelligence. Debt is a leverage system for the rich not a death trap. Using your money will not help you achieve what other people's money can through the power of leverage.

FOCUS

Financial intelligence gives you the power to control and use leverage. Financial intelligence requires focus and begins with what you want to leverage upon and what you are investing in. Most people invest for capital gains and cash flow in the business of money. You need to know which of them you are investing for . Failing to know is a celebration of ignorance and mediocrity.

CAPITAL GAINS

Many people are used to investing for capital gains. That's why they are afraid of taking risk to invest. Capital gains is risky as in some countries, investing for capital gains invites a tax increase. People think they are smart, that they are investing for gains unknown to them they are investing in vain. It is based on assumption and speculations.

CASH FLOW

Investing for cash flow has less risk. Cash flow investment is investing in cash flow. You can leverage on your bankers money for a higher return of investment and pay less in taxes. This is profitable leverage.

BUDGETING YOUR MONEY

Budget is a plan for your resources and expenditure. You will either use your budget plan to become richer or poorer. Many people operate their lives on budget deficit rather than a budget surplus. Instead of creating a budget surplus, many people work to live bellow their means, which often means creating a budget deficit. Baron's Finance and Investment handbook explains a budget deficit like this; " **Excess of spending over income, for government, cooperation or individual**." Identify these word **"excess of spending over income."**

REASONS

The reason so many people operate on a budget deficit is because it so easier to spend money than to make money. When people have problems with their budget they cut back on their spending thinking that's the right thing to do.

HOW TO KNOW A RICH AND A POOR PERSON

It's easier to distinguish a poor person from a rich person based on their money spending habits. Our expenses predict our future. What we spend our money and time on determines if we can get rich in life or stay poor. The financial problem for many people begins from their budgets and grow bigger when these problems are not properly solved.

RICH	POOR
Investing on financial education	Investing in musical shows and football tickets
Paying for investment and business seminars	Investing in beer and cigarettes
Books and handbooks	Cable bills
Health check up and Gym dues	Food and cloths
Personal coach	Friends

What you spend your time , money and the kind of people you spend your time with determines your financial future. Time and money are your greatest assets don't abuse it, use it wisely if you want to become rich. What we do frequently becomes a habit that sharpens our reality. Spend your time and money wisely and resourceful to become rich.

LEGALIZE YOUR MONEY

The sky is wide enough for the birds to fly. The government print and legalize their money. You can also print and legalize your money. This is not illegal money that could land you in jail. This is what the rich do that the poor and middle class don't. A high financial intelligence would empower you to print your money legally without working hard. The rich print their money legally through their assets. Their assets are their money printing machine. You can print your money legally and live larger than life. Each time I want to print more money I write a book like this and publish it and put it in the market or I establish a new business that will generate regular cash flow. If they government print their money autocratically you have the privilege to democratize it legally.

KEY POINTS

- ✓ If you want to beat the rich, you must learn, study and master these game of money called cash flow.
- ✓ The potential power of financial knowledge empowers you with the skill to turn thrash into cash.
- ✓ Most people will continue to suffer financial problems because they lack financial management skills.
- ✓ The power of monopoly is your ability to control your money directly without external interference. Monopoly makes the rich smarter and richer.
- ✓ Your ability to read figures will make you financially intelligent.

PART EIGHT

MIND YOUR OWN BUSSINESS

" Great spirits always face violent opposition from mediocre minds."

- Albert Einstein

If you don't mind your business in life, you will help people mind their business. Your business is what you do with your life, time, energy and money. I see people helping people take care of their business while they get poorer they make other richer with their time, energy and life. Your greatest assets in this information age is your time. How well do you invest your time and life in your business. A day gone is gone forever. If you cant invest your time in your business and future other will help you invest it in their business and future.

YOUR MAIN BUSSINESS

You main business is not to look what kind of business other people are doing, how much they are earning and how far they are going. Your business is to look after your business. Make impact with what you are good at and passionate about and maximize your destiny. Face your track and don't run on another man's track.

NO COMPETITION IN DESTINY

I saw a lorry carrying an inscription "No competition in destiny." While taking a ride around town. Life is not about competing with others but competing with yourself to be successful. Leave those that want to compete for money, power, fame and influence to keep competing. Don't be carried away by envy when you see people that you are better of getting ahead of you. "Envy is suicide" as advised by Tony Robbins. There are challenges that you must compete with not people.

NOT HOW FAR BUT HOW WELL

Life is not how far you can run but how well your life can become. In the story of the hare and tortoise which my mother told me as a child. The hare and the tortoise were competing for a race. The hare was far ahead of the tortoise. Along the way the hare got exhausted and decided to look for water to drink and rest for a while and eventually slept off. The tortoise that was miles away soon came and passed the hare and won the race smartly not hardly. It is through perseverance that the snail reached the ark. People that thought were ahead of me are now behind me. People that look down at you in a matter of time will bow down to you. Just stick to your dream and create a process that will work for you.

PROCESS TO SUCCESS

We all have process of becoming rich. Bill Gates founder of microsoft, Mark Zuckerberge founder of face book, Richard Branson founder of virgin airline, Donald Trump founder of Trump organization, Steve Jobs founder of Apple, Jeff Bezo founder of Amazon , Michael Dell founder of Dell computer and Tony Tunner founder of CNN all had their processes. If Robert Kiyosaki process of becoming rich was through real estate It might not work out well for me. My process of writing books, Hosting seminars and building and buying business might not work for you. You need to create your process to become rich.

THINK AND CREATE

If you can think and create you can become rich. I own a social network site where people can get socialized twinklenet.yooco.org This is a life time asset and investment that I have created through the power of creative thinking. It is a worldwide business that I am leveraging through the power of the web. I have blogs mickydia.blogspot.com,Superlearning.blogspot.com, where I educate and motivate people through my articles and an online magazine Myblogerzine .blogspot.com This is the power of building network.

NETWORK

What makes the rich successful is their network. Macclef law is based on the principle of multiplication. The more people that you have in your network will determine how richer you will become. The rich build networks that work like a train that carries many people. If you are smart to build a network around your idea and business you will become richer beyond your wildest dreams.

TAKE ACTION

You need to decide and take action about what you want in your life. You can keep your job and start a business no matter how small to gain the expertise and experience to start and build bigger business. Taking action is the first step towards achieving success. Any successful business that you see was a courageous step taken by someone. I keep telling people that instead of enriching someone business, Start your business to enrich your self. Failures and losers will never get ahead in life because their inability to take action over their life.

IT TAKES RESPONSIBILITY

Blaming is easy. But you don't have to keep nagging and complaining about why things are not working for you. Its time you grow up. Only babies nag and complain. If I had blamed the world, family and friends for not supporting my vision. I would never had achieved anything meaningful in my life. Its time you take full responsibility over your life and blaze your path to success.

BE TRUE TO YOUR SELF

Many people know the truth but they will never accept the truth. They prefer people that will keep telling them lies to extort money from them. And many keep lying to themselves failing to realize its implication. They know that they are working hard and not earning enough. Instead of starting a business to support them. They will say " Starting a business or investing is risky."

A young man approached me asking me what kind of business she should invest in or start. I told her to go and enroll in an investment and business class to learn. She replied; " I don't have all the time. I have enough money to invest and start a business." I gave her back her answer; " You have enough money to invest and start a business." I wished her good luck. She meet some bad advisers that told her to invest in product and a business which never got off the ground. Many people will keep failing because they refuse to learn. It is when you learn that will begin to earn.

LEARN TO EARN

It baffles me when I hear people complaining that they are not earning enough in their jobs and business and they not willing to do something about it. If you have a problem and you didn't take action do something about it. The problem will get bigger then you will not be able to control it. If you don't do something to solve your problems then something will do you. Just like a virus that attacks a laptop or computer if it is not attended to the virus will destroy the hard drive. That is how problems destroy people making them work harder and live harder. I don't just tell people to go and start a business over invest without learning the principles and gaining the education required to start, build and invest in a business. If you haven't learned how to crawl as a baby how would you have walked? As a teenager I accompanied my friends to the river to swim. I dived into the river and almost drowned because I haven't swarmed in my life. I need to learn the process. Failing to learn will only drown you more into your problems.

VALUE KNOWLEDGE THAN MONEY

People that value money than knowledge don't get ahead in life. They work and die as slaves for money struggling in financial hardship all their lives because of their ignorance. I have never worked for money. I rather work hard to gain knowledge than work for money. I have worked in places with the desire to gain knowledge not money. I wouldn't have been a computer guru if I hadn't worked for free at a small business center for a woman. I learned how to use and operate computer from her and keep developing my skills and opening my mind to learn more. It cost me less, because I couldn't afford to go to a computer institute. I do business on the web, write my book and sell on line, network with the experience I have acquired through valuing knowledge than money.

THE NEW MONEY

The world has changed from material to mental age. The new money of the information age is knowledge and information. It is not about the amount of money in your bank account that guarantee your financial freedom but the amount of knowledge in your brain and the information that you have. The greatest bankruptcy in the world is lack of knowledge. Prophet Hosea was right when he said" My people perish for lack of knowledge." Knowledge is the potential power that you need to break through the limitation of financial freedom. It is potential power that can make you get and achieve the possibility of your dreams. Albert Einstein said; " Nothing can withstand a man with knowledge." A man with knowledge is powerful to make and multiply his money. It is your knowledge about money that will ensure your survival in this volatile information age.

LAST LAUGH

I invested my years buying books and attending seminars. Many of my friends were making jest of me thinking I was wasting my time and money. They are fond of saying instead of me buying books I should be buying cloths and shoes. That is the way you identify poor people. They live for the moment and immediate gratification. The rich invest today, deny immediate gratification to reap their fruit of labour in the future. I have seen how far many of them have gone. I am now having the last laugh.

RESULTS TERMINATES INSULT

When people don't see results or something profitable in what you do. They will begin to grumble to discourage you. Success is a process not a get rich quick scheme. The result takes time to manifest. You just have to focus on your goal and don't give in to noisy criticism. I have never seen a critic that achieved a single thing in his life.

CHANGE YOUR REALITY

Whatever you have been told or taught affects your reality. If you want to start your life and recover from the mistakes that you've made you have to change your reality. Irrespective of whether you are educated or uneducated, Skilled or unskilled, Intelligent or unintelligent should affect your reality. Changing your reality is changing what you think, belief and yourself concept this affects your destiny and who you become in life.

TEACHING THROUGH MOTIVATION

It's my mission to advocate financial literacy and Life motivational education to motivate people to become financial successful. I discovered that our traditional school teaching style is based on fear and threats rather than motivation and encouragement. Students are punished for their mistakes instead of corrected for their mistakes. This is instills fear of failure in the minds of students and become part of them.

WORDS ARE LIFE

Words are life and powerful. When teachers call students failures it becomes a reality and affects their destiny. People that are afraid of taking risk and making mistakes are the biggest failures. Show me failure and I will show you a coward. The school train students to imitate rather than innovate. This is the reason why many students after graduating from school loss their inborn creativity that could help them become great in life

LIFE IS A GAME

Life is a game of winners and losers. Winners never quit, Losers rarely win. In the game of money the rich are the winners and the poor and middle class are losers. I am not insulting anybody but I am trying to make a point. In today's volatile economy and changing world the middle class and the poor are losers. They are been left behind with their obsolete ideas. They are ignorant of the idea of how money works. The only world that they know working hard for money. They will continue to struggle with their old rules of money mentality which becomes their reality. Such rules can't save them in this age and they are still advising their children to get academic qualification to get a good job, making them to walk in their pattern.

LAW BREAKERS

The rich live and act differently. They break the rules and create their rules that will work harder for them to get richer. They do not cling to the old rules of money like the poor and middle class does. Their rules make their money work hard for them instead. They use it to their advantage to maximize opportunities to print their money legally. The rich values financial intelligence and advise their children to learn how hard their money will work hard for them. That is a winning attitude in the game of money.

STOP WISHING DO SOMETHING

Stop wishing and dreaming and start doing something right from where you are with what you have. Theocritus advised; "Trying will do anything in this world." When you haven't tried to achieve what you want in life by taking the first step and working towards achieving your goal. You are only just dreaming. The world is filled with dreamers. Its time you stop dreaming and become a realist. I have heard people say these words; " I wish I can make more money." " I wish I can quit my job and start my own business." " I wish I can start investing for my future." Al this words will never come alive when you don't put it into physical action by doing something daily that will make your wishes a reality.

TEST OF CHARACTER

It is in times of adversity that we bring out who we really are. Warriors or cowards. Theodore Roosevelt asserted; " The chief factor in any man's success or failure must be his own character." Many people want the prize but they are not willing to pay the price to get the prize. There is no success without sweat. There is no victory without battle. I have fought hard and I am still fighting for what I want to achieve in life. I have experienced a life without money based on my reality. I have starved and slept in the streets of Lagos just because I have made up my mind to blaze my path to financial freedom by going on my own. I had opportunities presented to me to get high paying jobs but I refused to compromise the strength of my character. This journey has been a lonely road for me but I have to keep carrying my cross till I get to my promise land. It takes a determined spirit to survive and thrive in the game of life. No pain , no gain. When you see successful people and failures it lies in their strength of character. And your character is who you are and what you stand for. If you know what you are doing is right. You will want to fight a good fight to win. See you at the top.

KEY POINT

- ✓ If you can't invest your time in your business and future other will help you invest it in their business and future.
- ✓ You main business is not to look what kind of business other people are doing, how much they are earning and how far they are going. Your business is to look after your business.
- ✓ If you are smart to build a network around your idea and business you will become richer beyond your wildest dreams.
- ✓ Many people will keep failing because they refuse to learn. It is when you learn that will begin to earn.
- ✓ It is your knowledge about money that will ensure your survival in this volatile information age.
- ✓ People that are afraid of taking risk and making mistakes are the biggest failures.

PART NINE

GUIDE

TO FINANCIAL

FREEDOM

"If you know the way, you will get somewhere and if you don't you will get nowhere."

-Michael Ediale

The path to financial freedom is having total control over your life , time and money. Irrespective of been an employee, and self employed you can become financially free. Your chosen career path in the quadrant doesn't matter as long as you can manipulate the system by playing smartly in all the four quadrants.

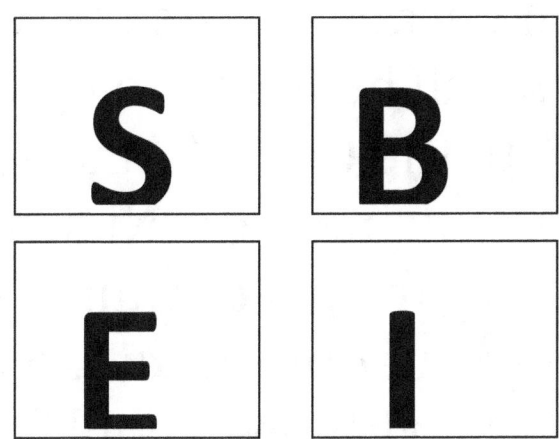

An employee while working can still own his private business , have other bigger business with smart employees managing it and still invest in other business. For example a nurse working in a hospital can own a pharmacy store and later own a hospital and hand it over to a smart doctor with nurses working for her weather she decides to work or not.

WE ALL NEED TO BE BUSSINESS PEOPLE

I was discussing with a college girl at a church about the benefits of been self employed. The lady asked me " Must everybody own a business? " She further added; " If everyone owns a business who are the people that will work." My answer to her goes like this; " We all need to have a business irrespective of whether we work or not." America is rich because of its free capitalist society that allows small business to thrive. Small business contribute to the GDP of American economy than bigger business do. Nigeria is in recession and suffering from a declining economy because we have more people interested in working for paychecks with few people owning businesses , creating and innovating great products and services. If everyone owns a business there will be an affordable standard of living and more taxes and revenue for the government to boost the economy and create more job opportunities.

IT'S TIME FOR BUSSINESS

Building a business is different from starting a business. These is the reason why nine out of ten business fails in less than five years. I have seen people wake up and start a business that never picks up from the ground. Many people think that the easiest way to financial freedom is to start a new business, product and a service. So they raise capital and start their own business and they soon start where they finish from. I was asked by a journalist what do I do for a living? I answered the young man by saying; " I am into the business of building businesses and creating jobs." If you want to go into business learn to build a business that can expand or you might just end up in the trap of been self employed. It's easier to start an ice cream stand in a the street compared to building an ice cream company.

SECRET SUCCESS OF THE RICH EXPOSED

The rich become richer through building business. Their business are assets that produce cash flow. They build business that people run for them without them working in the business.

Building a business is a guaranteed way to financial freedom not starting a business. As beautiful as it sounds, it's also the most difficult ways of getting rich. Building a business takes years, time, creativity and continuous learning.

IT'S ABOUT SYSTEMS

To become a successful business owner your major goal is to own a system and have people work that system for you. You can develop the business system yourself or you can purchase a system. A business that has no system will crash and never get off the ground. The hardest thing to build in a business is a system. If you have a faulty system and the people working in the system are faulty there is a problem. The rich focus more on the business system than the cash flow. System keeps a business moving. It's the life of the business. Just as an airplane it comprises of systems if one system gets faulty it would crash in the air.There are three kinds of business systems that can make you rich. They are:

1. Traditional business- Where you develop your own system
2. Franchises – Where you buy an existing system
3. Network Marketing: Where you buy into and become part of an existing system.

Buying an existing business system and joining a network marketing system are the easiest. Once you can get these systems all you need to do is to develop your people to operate on the system. The advancement in technology has reduced the risk s involved in owning a business. Anyone can own a business and become successful if they know what they are doing and leverage on the power of systems.

A NEW DAWN

Been broke, hungry and homeless was an event not an experience. My experience is in overcoming my adversity and rising to financial stability. True freedom and security is not found in what we have acquired in life but in what we know and what we can create with our talents.

Through the application of knowledge and maximizing my potentials I have successfully created a publishing company, Entertainment company, Education Company and Manufacturing company. I don't need to brag about my achievements but I want to use this medium to motivate you that you can achieve more if you can just apply the principles that you've learned in this book.

A WORLD WITH PROBLEMS

The world is filled with problems. Identify a need that you can provide or problems that you can solve. You are on your path to become a millionaire. The rich turn problems into business opportunities and becomes richer. Just a solution for a problem is capable of turning your life around.

TWO KIND OF PEOPLE WITH DIFFERENT MESSAGE

Entrepreneurs are not the only kind of people that discover and maximize opportunities to make profit. We have the propreneurs, these people respond to a higher calling, spending years sharpening their saw, and developing their potentials and delivering their service for free before they finally get their break. Artists, Athletes, writers and sages are propreneurs. I feel I belong to this group. I see my calling in life is to make impact that was why I wasn't discouraged when things where not going as I had expected for years. I see getting a job as a major distraction from fulfilling my destiny. I took it personal when people tell me to get a job. I would find all means to defend what I believe in. Proprenuers don't work for money but with time they become the richest. Entrepreneurs are out to make money and when the money is not coming forth they run into the safe umbrella of job security.

WHAT EFFECT DO YOUR PARENTS HAVE ON YOU?

Who are your parents and what impact have they made in your life? Are they pushing you towards job security or the path to financial freedom. My mother had a great impact in my life. I had watched her as a child and watch how prosperous she was. I wanted to prosper I decided to follow her steps to financial freedom. My dad was highly educated man that valued job security. By the time he realized it. The fairy tale was over. I would rather spend years building my ark than to help and waste my life building someone's ark.

THE ARK

Many people will drown in the flood because they didn't build their ark. They were happy receiving paycheck building other peoples ark and never bothered to build their ark. Just like the days of Noah many people will be drowned in the flood when they retire or loss their job without an ark to shield them. The earlier you start building your ark the better it would be for you.

EYES OF THE NEEDLE

I have been doing everything all by myself. Burning my energy, working hard to make money. Unknown to me I was a working slave . I was working hard for money and living hard even though I was self employed. I was the system of my business and sometimes when I get ill. I am out of business. I wanted to be rich and I have no valuable product or service that can serve more people without my effort. Until I wrote my books and other educational products and leveraged on amazon.com I passed through the eye of the needle. Making my products available worldwide, making money even when I sleep. Living a life without stress and having the time to think more creatively. That was how I passed through the eye of the needle. " Thinking is the hardest work there is. That is why so few people engaged in it."

BE THE BEST YOU WANT TO BE

To be rich and poor is a matter of choice. You have the right to decide whom you become. Your decisions becomes your reality which reflects your personality and predicts your destiny. You can be the best you want to be irrespective of your present situation in life. Don't look for the easiest road to success blaze your own path. You must follow the process I took. Create and think of the process that would favour you. There is always a light that shines at the end of the tunnel. I wish you good luck in your journey to financial freedom and I hope to see you at the top.

INVESTMENT

Everybody invests in different ways. The poor and middle class invest in their children education with the intension of been taken care of in the future when they get old by their children. Many work hard and save to buy a house and a car that is what they think is investment. If you want to be rich you must learn what the rich invest in and how they invest.

YOU CAN BECOME RICH BY INVESTING

Many people think that it takes money to invest. Yes that is true but your time and knowledge also requires investment. The problem with investment is that you might make money if you are financially educated and loss money if you are financially illiterate. If you lack the skills required to become an investor you will only experience pain than to gain. Your money can disappear in thin air than multiply. As we all know the stock market use to be the best investment for the rich and middle class until people began to lose their money. It became volatile and risky to venture into.

WHAT IT TAKES TO INVEST

It still takes money and financial education to invest. The rich take bankers money to invest and get richer . The real estate is a guaranteed investment. You can enroll into real estate classes to learn how to buy, sell and invest in real estate. You can browse through Richdad.com for more information. Robert Kiyosaki is a titian and educator in the real estate business. He has books and seminars that can help you invest and get richer in real estate.

FINANCIAL INDEPENDENCE MEAN DIFFERENT THINGS TO DIFFERENT PEOPLE

In the book; " Something for Nothing" Brain Tracy wrote about his experience from his focal point advanced coaching and mentorship program. He explained how an exercise was carried out in values clarification. A check of ten million dollars was given to everyone in the program which was not cashable. The idea of giving out the ten million dollar check was to give people the opportunity to fantasize about what they really want in their lives.

The participants were divided into groups to discuss what they would do if they suddenly received ten million dollars each. Then they report back to the group. It was recorded after the discussion that almost what the participants wanted in their lives doesn't cost any money. When people think about financial independence , they immediately think about quality of life issues. Many of the participants gave these answers; *" I would work shorter days and spend more evenings and weekends with my family; I would take a long vocation with my wife, I would join a health club and exercise everyday to lose weight and get fit. I would write a book I've always wanted to write, I would get involved in charity and church activities."* This is an exercise you can do as well, imagine you have received a ten million dollar check right now. What would you do differently in your life right now? Think about what you want in your life and begin to write it down.

KEY POINT

- ✓ Your chosen career path in the quadrant doesn't matter as long as you can manipulate the system by playing smartly in all the four quadrants.

- ✓ If everyone owns a business there will be an affordable standard of living and more taxes and revenue for the government to boost the economy and create more job opportunities.

- ✓ Building a business takes years, time, creativity and continuous learning.

- ✓ The rich focus more on the business system than the cash flow.

- ✓ Anyone can own a business and become successful if they know what they are doing and leverage on the power of systems.

- ✓ The earlier you start building your ark the better it would be for you.

- ✓ Don't look for the easiest road to success blaze your own path.

PART TEN

KIND

OF

MONEY

"Guard your integrity as a sacred thing; nothing is at last sacred but the integrity of your own soul."

-Ralph Waldo Emerson

SCHOOL OF LIFE

Everything that I do today was what live taught me not school. School only taught me how to spell bicycle but not to ride. School only taught me academic intelligence that would get me a job and taught me to work hard and compete for grades and awarded me with credentials making me believe that it would make me successful in real life. Life taught me how financial and emotional intelligence that would make me far more successful beyond credentials. School life is different from real life. School life is an event that comes and go but real life is a continuous school that never ends . The day we stop learning is the day that we start dying. School life forbids making mistakes but real life is a patient teacher that encourages mistakes. The school produces smart people but life produces smarter people. In real life I have seen A students work hard for school dropouts and C students. Real life makes the impossible possible and unbelievable believable.

IT'S ABOUT A MISSION

Everybody comes into life and passes out of life. There are some people that will never achieve anything great and never make impact in this life simply because they don't have a mission which they want to accomplish in life. Mission is the purpose of your journey in this life. Only people that discover and maximize their great vision becomes great in life.

FINDING MY MISSION

In life we are allowed to pass through many experiences because in it lives our mission. Our mission is to solve a problem. After been plagued by poverty since childhood, growing up on my own without a silver spoon doing anything that comes into my mind to do. Spending years doing different things I struggled because I had no mission in life. Without mission there is no domination and direction in life. At age 29 was when I discovered my true mission after the demise of my mother I knew I had to do something profitable with my life. A friend took me to a seminar where Nelson Mandela's documentary was played he made a statement that penetrated into my soul saying; " We humans have very little time on earth. Whatever you will do it quickly." He narrated how he discovered his mission to fight against appthied is South Africa and the difficulties he had to pass through to achieve his mission. That was the day I found my mission and I wrote it down; " To be a difference marker in the personal and professional lives of millions of people by liberating them from financial bondage and advocate financial literacy through motivational education." I have want to make people become rich by motivating them to achieve success. This mission guided me through the journey of life and has taken me this far changing the way millions of people think about life, money and success.

A VOW OF POVERTY

Many religious people have vowed to remain in poverty all their lives to fulfill their spiritual belief. I have heard people use words like; " I rather be happy than to be rich." " The love of money is the root of all evil." They think that money is not important in their life. What is important is their faith. Money is not everything. But I rather have money and be happy than to be happy and not have money. I have vowed never to be poor in my life that I the reason why I took a courageous step not to work for money but learn how to make for money. While growing up I have see how my father and mother quarrel and how my father lived in frustration because of money problems. I don't want to experienced the same family pattern that was the reason why I made up my mind and vowed to be rich.

POWER OF WORDS

I know how powerful words are. I have read the bible and knew that words are life and words become flesh. The word poverty doesn't exist in my vocabulary. When people tell me that I am broke I reject such statement by telling them that I am rich, I am a billionaire. People think that I am proud. I don't care what they think our difference is based on our mentality which becomes our reality. I have vowed to be rich and never to be poor in life.

INVINSIBLE MONEY

I call my self a billionaire even when I had no car, no physical money and I was struggling financially. What kept motivating me was the billions of dollars that I see with my mind eye which no one sees. These invincible money was what keep motivating me to unlock the potentials in me to make it a reality. As Robert Collier puts it; *"Whatever the mind can conceive and perceive it can achieve."*

WHAT KIND OF MONEY TO YOU WANT IN LIFE

We all need money and work for money. But which money are you working for? Which money do you want to make you rich, comfortable and secured in life. There are three kinds of money that people work for . They are:

1. Competitive money

2. Cooperative money

3. Spiritual money

COMPETITIVE MONEY

This is the type of money that the school train people to compete for just as they are trained to compete for grades, jobs and promotions. This is the game of survival for the fittest. Most people with academic qualifications work for competitive money.

COOPERATIVE MONEY

This is the type of money acquired from team work which is derived from sports and in business. This is what the most powerful entrepreneurs build by establishing a cooperation. Their cooperative team makes them more competitive. This is the money of great leaders which they execute through their teams. Most entrepreneurs of large are great team leaders.

SPIRITUAL MONEY

This is the best form of money which someone can work for. It is type of money that is derived from responding to a higher calling. This is not restricted to church and charity alone. Working for spiritual money is not about working to get paid but it is about working for free to fulfill a purpose of existence. This is where the power of mission attracts mission enablers to support your mission and open doors of opportunities for you in course of performing your life task.

ARE YOU MAXIMIZING YOUR GIFT

We all have special gifts, have you discovered and start maximizing your gifts. Your wealth is in your gifts and talents not credentials. Credential is not potential. Every talent you have is meant to make you rich and enrich the lives of others. Most people are talented but they don't want to work hard to develop and maximize it. This is one of the reasons why many people remain average and unsuccessful. A man's talent makes way for him to be rich. It's my talent for writing that had made me written books that has enriched people's lives and also enriched me in the process. Let people see the value in your talent.

TALENT IS NOT ENOUGH

It's not about been talented in a particular skill. It's about developing, mastering your talent and maximizing it effectively. The world is filled with talented poor people. John C Maxwell wrote a potential effectiveness book titled; *Talent is not enough.* I will recommend you read this book. Great doctors spend years in school and then practice for years developing their gifts, Great golfers, artistes, artist, writers, athletes have been practicing their skills for years, developing their talents before having their break. That is one of the reasons why they are highly paid. Jim Collins book *Good to Great* will help you become the best you want in life.

DARE TO BE DIFFERENT

The best way for your life and business to thrive is to set yourself apart. Dare to be different. Do what no other business can do. This will give you a high competitive advantage from competitors. Leverage on your competitive advantage to grow and expand your business.

WHY DEPEND ON THE GOVERNMENT?

I have made up my mind after watching my late dad depended on the government all his life time and he was disillusioned. I feel and have concern for people who are still depending on the government to take care of them for life. That is what motivates me to write books and life educative products such as audio, and videos because we are in the information age the idea of job security and retirement benefits for life died with the industrial age. That was what my late dad realized in 1989 when he retired was the same year the world changed into the information age. My concern is that many people are not prepared to survive in this information age. The idea of going to school, get a high paying job and expect retirement benefits for life is not applicable in this information age. Education is still important but we must know how to invest and keep increasing our financial intelligence. Investment and Financial intelligence are not subjects taught in school. One of the greatest problem and dangers is that too many people have become dependent on the government to solve their personal problems. In 2020 the dependence on the government will be higher from the unemployed, employed and retirees. My fear is that the government will not be able to solve their problems and the problems will become bigger. Every government that comes into power introduces promises to make them popular. And people invest in their promises for social security and welfare. There have been unfulfilled promises that had been made and the promises keep coming and going. I don't think this promises will ever be fulfilled. It only make the people hopeless. Our government is beginning to increase taxes to enrich some people and impoverish the masses. Why depend on people who don't care about you? Depend on yourself and take responsibility for your life today. Instead of learning to save, learn to invest.

RISK THE RISK

People who will never take risks can't change their situation or change their world. Risk takers are world changers. Can the government take care of your risk in this information age? The times are changing, running the government is becoming expensive but many people are still obsolete with the idea of entitlement. President Buhari promise of 5,000NGN benefits for the poorest Nigerians and feeding of school children daily is an obsolete idea of the industrial age. The times are changing but our political leaders are not. They are still clinging to old ideas of the industrial age. It's no more the responsibility of the government, union, and family to take care of you when your working days are over. If you think I am wrong please you can stop reading this book right here. It is my concern for people that want to take the risk to take charge of their financial lives, future and destiny but who do not know how to begin. It takes courage to make the right move. If you are comfortable with your financial life. "Congratulations" and if you have not you've found the right book that would place you from financial adversity to stability.

FREEDOM DOESN'T MEAN FREE

For every freedom is a price to be paid. Mahatma Ghandi didn't achieve his quest for freedom for India for free. Nelson Mandela didn't achieve freedom from apartheid in South Africa for free. Martin Luther King Jr didn't achieve his struggle on racial discrimination in America for free. Financial freedom might be free, but it does not come cheap. Freedom has a price to be paid. Jesus Christ was crucified and his blood was shed on the cross of Calvary to redeem and free mankind from sins. Freedom is worth the price if it must be achieved.

WHAT DOES IT TAKES TO BE FREE?

The biggest lies that people believe and that has held them captive is that it takes money to be financially free, It takes a high paying job and a good formal education to be financially free. These are wrong advices to achieving true financial freedom. Dreams, desire, determination and persistence are required to achieve financial freedom.

WHAT WE ARE TAUGHT TO BELIEVE

Our beliefs reflects our realities and sharpens our future. Job security is what many people seek because that is what they were conditioned to seek, at home and at school. Many people will keep accepting such believes no matter what you tell them. Many of us have been programmed from our early age to think about job security than financial security or financial freedom. What do you expect people who had never been taught about money at homes and school to do when they grow up with such believe. A teenage girl meet me and was complaining that she wants to study English language at the university but her mother was told that people who study English end up as primary school teachers. And, she began to disturb her daughter to choose another field to study preferable medicine. The mother wants job security for her daughter. These is what many people were taught to believe that is why they cling even tightly to the idea of job security instead of exploring financial freedom.

ARE YOU A BANK?

Many people have the habit of borrowing money from friends, families and relatives to take care of their financial problems. You don't have to give your money out to anybody that approaches you with their personal problems. You are not a bank to issue out loans. Must money given out to family and friends break up relationships and friendship when you need your money and they didn't comply. You can give from your heart to assist but don't borrow your money out. It creates problems. Only banks borrow people money.

FINANCIAL GOALS

Set up a financial goal for where you want to be in 5 years and a smaller, short –term financial goal for where you want to be in 12 months. Set goals that are realistic and attainable.

KEY POINTS

✓ School life is different from real life. School life is an event that comes and go but real life is a continuous school that never ends . The day we stop learning is the day that we start dying.

✓ Many of us have been programmed from our early age to think about job security than financial security or financial freedom.

✓ Freedom is worth the price if it must be achieved.

PART ELEVEN

SHARPEN
THE
AXE

"Opportunity is missed by most people because it is dressed in overalls and looks like work. "

- Thomas Edison

CATCHING A MONKEY

Asian and African natives have used this smart technique to catch monkeys for centuries. The hunter will find a tree with a small hole in the tree and place nuts inside the hole. A monkey will come and put its hand in the hole to grab onto the nuts. The monkey fist now clenched tight to the nuts cannot be withdrawn from the hole, trapping the monkey. Rather than let go off the nuts, the monkey will twist and turn but refuse to let go off the nuts in the hole until the hunters will return to capture or kill the monkey.

MONKEY MENTALITY

Humans are similar to monkeys. Many humans have the monkey mentality. Rather than cling to job security, their possessions and money. Humans are trapped like monkeys as they cling tighter to job security, benefits and money because they lack financial education. Like trapped monkeys in the tree, most people will spend their lives as wage slaves and tax slaves to their employees and the government.

A STATE OF CONFUSSION

Many people are confused just like the monkey turning and twisting still clinging to nuts in the tree refusing to let go to be free. Many people don't know what to do despite been aware of the economic and financial crisis catching up with them unprepared. Rather than let go old ideas they still cling tighter to their jobs hoping their political leaders would save their personal financial situation. Many think the solution to their financial problems is to go back to school to get higher qualification to get promotion and pay rise. Some know that they must make changes to survive this turbulent times. But their level of financial illiteracy and ignorance is trapping them just like a monkey in the tree.

RELICS OF THE PAST

From 2010 to 2020 the world has been experiencing the most volatile changing era in world history. Instead of evolving with the trend many people are still clinging to the relics of the past such as job security, saving money in the bank and depending on retirement benefits and entitlement for life. These are the people that are victims of the economic shipwreck revolving across the globe.

CRYSTAL BALL

Through the crystal ball we can predict the past, present and future. The gap between the poor and the rich has widened since 2010 and its getting wider in 2020. Many middle class people have slip into poverty line of the poor. The gap between the haves and hav-not has increased and it will keep increasing. The world will be filled with more poor people. The cause of this shift is not just lack of financial intelligence alone, but inflation and taxes. This will be a great era for the financial literate to get richer and a major problem for those with limited financial education.

FOR ONES PAIN

One of the problems with traditional education is the absence of real-life experience. Many students graduate from school with technical answers to problems but lack the skills required to put their technical knowledge into proper use. In this era of economic upheaval many graduates are leaving school but not finding jobs. It is this real world experience that is important to a person's life ling learning and personal development that defines who they become in life. It's not about whom you know, what you know but who you are that really counts.

TEACHERS &MENTORS

Many students' most important mentors and instructors are their teachers, who have trained them to find jobs than create jobs, consume than to create products and services, save than to invest. These are the traits of an employee. They are deficient of real- life skills to become an entrepreneur. Beware of who your teachers and mentors are. I tried to get some mentors but I have to drop them because they are employees and I am an entrepreneur. Our reality differs. I found mentors in books and learn from their success and failures.

CREDENTIAL IS NOT POTENTIAL

Many people cling to their credentials like the monkey cling to nuts. Without getting a job they look miserable and useless. Credential is just a report card for completion of a particular field of study from the school. It has limitation of how successful it can make you in real-life. I have seen people with great portfolio of credentials working hard for school dropouts who looked beyond their credentials and developed their potentials to become rich and successful in life. You go to school to get a profession as a doctor or lawyer but you do not go to school to be rich or become an entrepreneur. Some of the richest smartest people in the world didn't do well in school or had great credentials from reputable universities. Examples are Henry Ford, founder of Ford; Thomas Edison, founder of General Electric, Mark Zuckerberge, founder of Facebook; Richard Branson, founder of Virgin; Walt Disney, founder of Disney world; Bill Gates, founder of Microsoft; Michael Dell, Founder of Dell computers and Steve Jobs, founder of Apple. In this changing world your potential will make you rich not your credential.

TIME TO LET GO

A monkey that is trapped cannot find freedom until the monkey lets go to what he is clinging to. We cannot find freedom while we are still clinging to old , obsolete ideas. Rigid minded people will continue to struggle. People who keep doing the same thing, in the same way, over and over again and expecting a different result are out of their minds. This act is tantamount to insanity. People who keep listening to obsolete ideas from teachers, advisers and mentors will continue to cling to those old ideas. Just as you can't teach an old dog new trick, it is also difficult to change a person who cling to obsolete ideas.

AN OPEN MIND WINS

This is the greatest time in world history for the open minded. People who are prepared to open their mind to new ideas and learn new ideas win and those with closed mind fail. Irrespective of been educated or uneducated, smart or not smart , rich or poor if you have a learnable spirit with an open mind you can change your world, life and future. It's easier to get richer if you will adopt new ideas and take your financial education seriously.

MY CONCERN

I have great concern for the world. I don't want to be selfish with the financial knowledge that I have acquired within the years. This is a way of giving back to the society what I have achieved that made me successful. I have concern for you reading this book to elevate your financial well-being. I have shared the secrets and principles in this book. I easy to show you a bicycle but its left for you to ride. Ride you way through road to financial freedom.

MORE THAN A BOOK

This book is beyond theory but real –life experience about what the street and life has taught me. My thoughts, actions, philosophy and experiences are covered in this book. I am offering you an idea to look at the subject of money in a simple and interesting way that will make a difference in your life. You can recommend this book to anyone that wants to improve their financial education.

A CALL OF ACTION

The personal and global financial crisis affecting us all will not be solved by the government and our political leaders. These crisis will continue until our schools embrace the necessity for financial education and begin to teach students about making money than working for money. These crisis will not stop until our students are been told the truth behind job security, working hard, paying high taxes and saving. Its time our school start training students to be creative, innovative and business wise. Its time our schools start letting go old ideas of the industrial age and accepting new ideas of the information age. If we don't teach people about the secrets of making money the more poor people we will have that will be depending on the government to take care of their financial problems. It is the power of financial education that can set everyone free. Knowledge is the real money if you gain knowledge from this book you are rich.

POWER OF FINANCIAL EDUCATION

True education empowers somebody to make impact in the world and create wealth. I have seen people who claimed to be highly academically educated struggling in real life because they lack the power of financial education. Turning information into a meaningful knowledge is the essence of education. How many people are maximizing the power of their education? Without financial education many people are just like empty barrels.

PAVLOVIAN DOGS

The Pavlovian dogs are trained to do as they are trained to do. Hit the plate and the dogs will begin to salivate even when there is no food. These is similar to millions of people that has been conditioned like the pavlovian dogs, doing as they are trained to do. Once the bell rings, employees find a high paying job and turn their money over to the banks and government.

NOT TOO LATE TO BEGIN

" What can I do? Is it too late for me to start over?" There is possibility to start life all over irrespective of your age. As long as you will be humble to learn through the process. At age 66, Colonel Sanders started all over and his humility to learn through the process created Kentucky Fried Chicken which grew to become an international business.

LESSON TO LEARN

He went broke when a new highway by passed his single store fried-chicken business. Once he saw how much his social security check was, he knew he was in trouble. So he packed his bags and began selling the rights to his special recipe to restaurants across the United States. He was turned down over 1.000 times before someone finally said yes. That led to his franchise operation. He took it public on the stock exchange, and he became a rich man. Today, Kentucky Fried Chicken is all over the world that has made other people rich.

CAN I DO THE SAME?

Thinking of an idea is easy but making it become money is not an easy task. The world is filled with hungry idealist that lack the capacity to make it a reality. You could learn from the failures and success of great entrepreneurs like Colonel Sander and Henry Ford. Education is important for everything but not for anything. What you need is a different kind of education that you can't find in the traditional school. That is the school of money.

SECRET - DIFFERENCES BETWEEN SCHOOLING & EDUCATION

Schooling is not education as many people think. Schooling does not necessarily produce rich , smart and wise people. Education always produce very rich, smart and wise people. Schooling prepares people for a career while education is an art of continuous learning to acquire information. schooling produces certificate holders and problems; education produces great achievers and problem – solvers. Schooling is made obligatory by society for everybody class; education is a mere choice made by lonely somebody. Investment in schooling produces paltry returns on investment; investment in education produce unimaginable huge returns on investment.

schooling produces career – servants who are stuck to the rat race and are grossly dependent, helpless when out of their jobs; education produces wealth–creators who are hardworking, creative, calculated risk-takers, problem-solving, enterprising and are massively independent – financially and lifestyle. Schooling takes more time to train you to becomedependent and poor; education takes littles or negligible time to train and make you become independent and wealthy! schooling is pursued and attended in an organized, formal, structured, popular, fanciful and regulated setting and atmosphere; education is pursued and acquired in an unorganized, informal, frustrating, unpopular, unstructured and most humbling setting and atmosphere. schooling success are taught by teachers produced within the same school system; education success is taught by coaches and mentors who had, have and are still product of the education setting and atmosphere. Schooling is man-made. the school system any where in the world is created by those who have education on how to be independent and successful; education is divinely endorsed by almighty god. reading and studying has divine endorsement – remember god is the first writer ofthe 10 commandments and he made his laws, ways, teachings and signs made to mankind through education (inspired writings, revelations, etc to his chosen prophets including Jesus christ , Muhammad , Buddha, Confucius) therefore, i challenged you this day henceforth, to dare to be educated rather than being schooled. 'study to show thyself approved' as instructed by almighty god in the holy bible (2 timothy 2:15). reading and studying (education) will equip you with functional, practional information that will transform your career, business and life beyond human imagination. it will help you rub mind with greater minds that can make you hot, sound and successfull

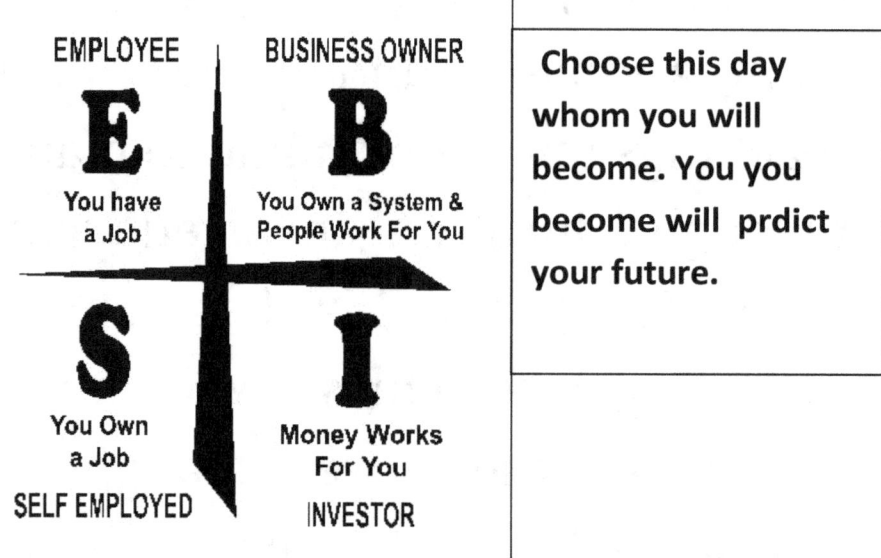

People who Say this can not be done should not interupt those doing it!

FIRST THINGS FIRST

Opportunities come and go in life. Some people seize it, enjoy the benefits and never look back, and majority simply just watch opportunities pass them by what will you do? The secret of getting ahead is getting started. Because those who do nothing today, end up being nothing tomorrow. Success comes to the man who does today what others think of doing tomorrow. The future never just happened, it was created. So, the way to have a better tomorrow is to start working on something worthwhile today.

YOUR NEXT STEP

It's now time to do the hardest thing : taking action.If you do the right thing now and take required actions, you are liberating yourself from financial hardship for life.You must know that every decision comes with a price.Today is the much dreamt and talked about future you have been expecting these past years. And are you really happy with your situation or condition today?

Your future happiness, fulfilment and financial empowerment lies with you this moment, so consider it carefully and take immediate action. Now is the right time to re-write the financial outcome of your future. Do not delay or procrastinate.

ACT NOW !

KEY POINTS

- ✓ Humans are trapped like monkeys as they cling tighter to job security, benefits and money because they lack financial education.

- ✓ The gap between the poor and the rich has widened since 2010 and its getting wider in 2020. Many middle class people have slip into poverty line of the poor.

- ✓ We cannot find freedom while we are still clinging to old , obsolete ideas.

- ✓ Turning information into a meaningful knowledge is the essence of education.

PART TWELVE

CAPITALISIM

MY STAKE

Capitalism has been attacked by many people who believe capitalists are corrupt, greedy and evil. True capitalist only profit when they help to make peoples life better, saving time and money through providing valuable services and products. I can fly safely, make phone calls, browse and make use of the computer to write books for people to read because some courageous capitalists made it easier and cheaper. I am able to do business with ease across the globe through the web. How can the capitalist that made life more pleasurable and simple be evil, greedy and corrupt. What about the people that exploit the capitalist system they are lazy, corrupts and greedy.

The school system has failed to teach and focus on true capitalism. Our system constitutes corrupt incompetent business and political leaders who have corrupted true capitalism. In the world today we have many civil servants and professional politicians without any real world business experience dominating the biggest business in the world. That is the business of government. This justifies why the government is corrupt. Like a cancer, legalized corruption eats away the fabrics of the world. This is the reason why men and women of power engage in power tussle and stealing the wealth of the people they are to serve.

Socialist is given a fair consideration. This is a system that steals from the poor to make the rich richer through taxes. Your cake belongs to everybody so it should be shared equally . While their cake belongs to them. This is evil, greedy and unfair. Our school advocates a socialist agenda making the rich look greedy and the poor needy. In Marxist theory, the proletariat is a class of capitalist society that does not have ownership of production. All they have to sell is their labor for a wage. Proletarians are wage –workers trained to work hard for money. Our school operates on these system of capitalism, the proletariat class, a wage earner, a person who leaves school looking for a job. These means many will never own anything of value , and many will die with nothing, simply because our schools, while resenting the rich, produce the workers they claim the rich exploit.

WHATS IN A JOB?

Many people that work hard for money or students that graduate from school looking for job think that their job is an asset. That is a mediocre thinking. A job cannot be passed to your kids, you cannot own a job for life and a job is not an asset.

WHATS IN MONEY

Working hard for money is just slavery. How can you be working for a money that is not an asset. It doesn't take money to make money and it can never take money to make money. With the rate of currency devaluation there is no longer value in a money. Money is idea, knowledge and information.

WHATS IN YOUR RETIREMENT PLAN?

I feel sorry for people that waste their lives working hard hoping to depend on their retirement plan after their working days are over. Your retirement plan is not an asset but an unfunded liability. Your retirement savings goes to the pocket of the rich through the government and financial institution who use your money very smartly to acquire great assets that makes them richer. They are using your money to get richer.

WEB OF CAPITALISM

Many students soon after leaving school looking for jobs are caught up in the web of capitalism. The school system failed to prepare students for real world not because they consider capitalism to be evil. Without any sound financial education, students are trained to be victims of capitalism. The ideology of the rich been greedy and exploitive becomes a reality. True capitalist are generous and prosperous because they produce a lot and receive a lot. Is the school system part of the conspiracy against capitalism?

CAPITALIST ALWAYS WINS

In the world of new economy there is always and will always be war for high wages verses low wages The capitalist class will always win because it is easy to move production to lower-wage nations. Technology also reduces the number of workers needed to run a business. Production goes up and labor costs go down. This make the capitalist win and thrive.

STILL IN THE DAR K AGES

The world is changing but our schools are not. They are still in the dark ages of industrial age. Our school continue to train and teach students to be proletarians, to leave school in search of high paying jobs. This is financial genocide which the schools should be held accountable for.

BEAR IN MIND

Always remember that in Marxist theory, the proletariat is a class of capitalist society that does not have ownership of the means of production. In the new economy, where money is no longer real money, the working class works in vain for nothing. They have no assets. A job is not an assets, money and retirement plan. It is a source of cash for true capitalists. When market crash, workers lose and capitalist wins.

RUNNING OR GROWING

Many people claim to be into business. That's a courageous step. But a question you should ask yourself is these: " Are you running or growing a business.?" Running a business is about running directionless for something probably money. Business that run after money soon run out of money. This is what many business people do thinking they are smart. The focus their attention on money accumulation. That is why many people think business success is an overnight phenomenon. This is a suicide mission leading to nowhere. Growing a business like planting a seed, watering and nurture it to grow. A farmer needs time, patience, discipline and faith to produce crops. That is how life in business should be.

SOWING AND REAPING

I don't believe in reaping without sowing. Sowing comes before reaping. This is a universal philosophy in life. You must sow into your life, financial education and business. I assure you it's not an easy task but it's worth the price. What you sow into your life today is what the future will bring fort.

KEY POINTS

- ✓ True capitalist only profit when they help to make peoples life better, saving time and money through providing valuable services and products.

- ✓ A job cannot be passed to your kids, you cannot own a job for life and a job is not an asset.

- ✓ With the rate of currency devaluation there is no longer value in a money. Money is idea, knowledge and information.

- ✓ Your retirement savings goes to the pocket of the rich through the government and financial institution who use your money very smartly to acquire great assets that makes them richer.

- ✓ Technology also reduces the number of workers needed to run a business. Production goes up and labor costs go down.

ABOUT THE AUTHOR

Michael Ediale is a success leader, author, financial educator and life motivator. His pattern of teaching has influenced the way many people think about life, money and success. He advocates financial literacy and motivational education through his writings . He has authored several books which are international sold on amazon.com. His mission is to liberate people from financial bondage and motivate them to become successful, richer and happier in life.

GET OTHER BOOKS

BY

MICHAEL EDIALE

➢ **Great Minds Think Great**
➢**Think Like The Rich**
➢**Passion Is The Key**
➢**Naira Crisis**
Available on Amazon.com
Login to place your order.

Must Read Books for you.

ACKNOWLEDGEMENT

I want to used this medium to acknowledge great authors whose books have motivated me to become successful and made this project a reality. Robert Kiyosaki, the author of Rich Dad ,Poor Dad you are a mentor and your knowledge has elevated my financial well-being. Tony Robbins, Brain Tracy, Jim Collins, your books have brought out the best in me and I am sharing the knowledge that I have acquired to the world.

Super learning International

Periodic Seminar / Business Presentation / Mentorship & Financial Intelligence

We encourage you to invite your friends, family, colleagues, neighbours to attend one of our periodic seminars and presentations at a venue close to you in your locality to learn more about achieving financial freedom through **Superlearningonline.blogspot.com facebook.com/Superlearningonline +2348175117119**

SCHOOL OF MONEY